WALTERS

MW01672212

WORDBOOK 6

Johnson O'Connor Research Foundation, Inc.
Vocabulary Building Program

By Richard Bowker

Vocabulary Scale 6915–7850
(Old VS 124–174)

Johnson O'Connor Research Foundation, Inc.

Atlanta • Boston • Chicago • Dallas • Denver • Houston
Los Angeles • New York • San Francisco • Seattle • Washington, D.C.

3/17

WORDBOOK
347 Beacon Street
Boston, MA 02116
(800) 355–3670

books@jocrf.org

The Johnson O'Connor Research Foundation, Inc. is a nonprofit scientific and research organization with two primary commitments: to study human abilities and to provide people with a knowledge of their aptitudes that will help them in making decisions about school and work. Since 1922, hundreds of thousands of people have used our service to learn more about themselves and to derive more satisfaction from their lives. The Foundation has offices in major cities across the nation. For more information about the aptitude testing program, go to http://www.jocrf.org, or contact any of our offices below.

Atlanta	(404) 261–8013	atlanta@jocrf.org
Boston	(617) 536–0409	boston@jocrf.org
Chicago	(312) 787–9141	chicago@jocrf.org
Dallas	(972) 991–8378	dallas@jocrf.org
Denver	(303) 388–5600	denver@jocrf.org
Houston	(713) 462–5562	houston@jocrf.org
Los Angeles	(213) 817–6625	la@jocrf.org
New York	(212) 269–0550	ny@jocrf.org
San Francisco	(415) 772–9030	sf@jocrf.org
Seattle	(206) 623–4070	seattle@jocrf.org
Washington, DC	(202) 828–8378	washdc@jocrf.org

ISBN 0-915212-05-6
Printed in the United States

Contents

How to Use This Book

This book has been written to help you increase your knowledge of words. It does this by discussing and testing you on words that are at a certain level of difficulty on our vocabulary scale. You have probably already taken a test which showed you where you score on this scale. If you study the words which are about at your level, they should be easier for you to learn than words that are much higher on the scale.

There are many different ways of using this book. If you are studying vocabulary as part of a class, your teacher may tell you the best way he or she has found to use it. If you are studying on your own, here are some suggestions:

> Start at the beginning of the book, even if it is below your vocabulary scale score. If you do not know some words below that level you certainly should learn them, and they should not be too difficult to learn.
>
> The first step in studying a chapter is to take the Pretest. This will tell you what words you do not know. You should certainly study any words you get wrong on this Pretest. Since it is possible to get an item right by guessing, you should also make a note of any words you aren't quite sure of; study them even if you get them right.
>
> Next, read over the discussion of each word you missed or weren't sure of. Memorize its meaning. Pay careful attention to the way the word is used in the sample sentences. Try to get a *feel* for the word. Use a dictionary (or two) in addition to reading the discussion. Try to understand the other forms which the word may take. (The lists of prefixes and suffixes at the end of the book can be very helpful for this.) When you think you know the word, go on to the exercises.
>
> The exercises give you three ways of testing your understanding of the word. They do not have to be done in any particular order. If you make a mistake on any one of them, though, you should go back and reread the discussion for that word. After every three chapters there is a review section for words in those chapters. Any words you get wrong on this review section should, of course, be restudied.
>
> You might want to work with the test words in other ways as well. Have someone read the words aloud to you; see if you can recognize them and write them correctly. Try to write a composition that uses all of the words. See if you can write good definitions of the words without looking at the discussions or a dictionary.
>
> Once you think you have learned the words in a chapter, go on to the next one. It is a good idea, though, to make a list or keep a notebook of the words you have learned so that you can review them from time to time. As you go through the book you may find the words becoming slightly more difficult. This will be particularly true as you go beyond your score on the vocabulary scale. If you get to a point where you are missing about half the words in a chapter, you should slow down and spend more time with each word. It would also be a good idea to begin studying the words that you got right on the Pretest, in order to fix them more firmly in your mind.

By the time you finish this book we hope that all the words in it will be a part of your vocabulary. At that point you should be ready to learn more words that are harder than these. You should continue to review these words, however, until you know them so well that they are a natural part of your speech and writing.

Chapter 1

Pretest

Each test word is printed in CAPITAL letters in a phrase. From the five choices on the next line, select the one which comes nearest in meaning to the meaning of the test word. Underline the one you select.

1. To LEVY a fine.
   increase | ignore | impose | accept | give back
2. Another ONSLAUGHT.
   arrival | argument | attack | death | victory
3. THWART his effort.
   delay | block | support | dislike | twist
4. Started to DEGENERATE.
   worsen | leave | fall | disappear | improve
5. Among the ELITE.
   last | worst | chosen | happiest | rest
6. Completely INDIFFERENT.
   separate | unaware | involved | similar | uninterested
7. KALEIDOSCOPIC events.
   publicly seen | important | faraway | strange | continually changing
8. PATERNAL cares.
   brotherly | inherited | motherly | continual | fatherly
9. In RETROSPECT.
   review | admiration | sight | planning | politeness
10. Sudden TORRENT.
   fire | flood | silence | fear | wind
11. Approached the ZENITH.
   bottom | wizard | peak | radio | end
12. They were BIGOTED.
   open-minded | intolerant | worried | vicious | greedy
13. They were EXCEPTIONAL.
   unnecessary | perfect | unusual | unfair | normal
14. IMPERATIVE statements.
   urgent | tender | royal | harsh | pleading
15. To PERCEIVE them.
   describe | show | hide | trick | notice

LEVY (lev′-E) v.: to impose, collect; to carry on (war)

To LEVY is to impose something like a tax or a fine, and to collect it by authority or force.

"The king LEVIED a new tax on the citizens."
"The judge LEVIED a huge fine on the company."

LEVY is also used in a different sense, to mean "to start or make war."

"The king decided to LEVY war against his enemies."

As a noun, a LEVY is the act of imposing or the thing imposed, a *tax*.

"The governor announced a new LEVY on cigarettes."

ONSLAUGHT (on′-slôt) n.: an attack, assault

ONSLAUGHT is related to the word *slaughter*. An ONSLAUGHT is a furious attack, of an enemy or of something like an enemy.

"The enemy launched a fierce ONSLAUGHT against our army."
"The ONSLAUGHT of the illness put him in the hospital for a week."
"They built a wall to protect themselves from the ONSLAUGHT of the cold wind."

THWART (thwôrt) v.: to block, prevent, foil, frustrate

To THWART someone is to block or prevent him from doing something. THWART suggests making things difficult for a person by running counter to what he wants or plans.

"The governor successfully THWARTED his opponent's attempt to win the election."
"Her plans to attend the party were THWARTED by a sudden illness."
"The baby screams whenever he is THWARTED"—that is, whenever he is not allowed to do something he wants to do.

In the Pretest, many people select *delay* as the meaning of THWART, but THWART suggests more complete and successful interference.

"Lack of funds *delayed* the project, but the principal's opposition finally THWARTED it."

DEGENERATE (di-jen′-ə-rAt) v.: to worsen, decline, deteriorate

To DEGENERATE is to become worse, to pass from a higher state to a lower or worse one. See *de-* under Prefixes. The word can be used about physical, mental, or moral qualities.

"The disease caused his health to DEGENERATE and now he's confined to bed."
"The play started brilliantly, but then DEGENERATED into a typical silly comedy."
"The once great lawyer has DEGENERATED into a drunken bum."

DEGENERATE is also an adjective and a noun, pronounced di-jen′-ə-rit. These words are most often used about lowered moral qualities.

"He may once have been a good man, but now he is just a DEGENERATE."
"The DEGENERATE emperor practiced every sort of vice."

ELITE (i-lEt′) n.: the chosen ones, a superior or highly special group

Note the pronunciation. ELITE originally came from a Latin word meaning to *choose*. The ELITE are the chosen ones, a group of people who are considered superior because of their achievements, wealth, power, or other quality.

"This store would only do business with the social ELITE."
"His tremendous feats as a hitter put him among baseball's ELITE."
"He was part of the political ELITE who ran the country year after year."

ELITE is also used as an adjective, meaning *choice* or *best*.

"An ELITE group of soldiers was selected to lead the attack."

Other forms of the word: ELITISM, n.
ELITIST, adj., n.

INDIFFERENT (in-dif′-ə-rənt or in-dif′-rənt) adj.: uninterested, unconcerned, unimpressive, commonplace

The most common meaning of INDIFFERENT is "not caring one way or the other"; in this sense the word is usually followed by *to.*

"I love swimming, but I am INDIFFERENT to winter sports."

"How can you be so INDIFFERENT to the suffering of these people?"

Another meaning of INDIFFERENT is "neither good nor bad," *commonplace, mediocre.*

"It was an INDIFFERENT novel; I've read much better."

"He played the piano very well, but he sang INDIFFERENTLY."

Other forms of the word: INDIFFERENCE, n.

RETROSPECT (re′-trə-spekt) n.: a review

RETROSPECT comes from a Latin word meaning to *look back at.* The *spect* part is also found in other words having to do with seeing, like *inspect* and *spectacles.* A RETROSPECT is a view of past events. The word is usually used in the phrase "in RETROSPECT," which means *in review, in looking back.*

"In RETROSPECT, I guess I made a mistake in doing what I did."

"At the time we thought we had failed, but in RETROSPECT it seems that we did pretty well."

Other forms of the word: RETROSPECTION, n.
RETROSPECTIVE, adj., n.

KALEIDOSCOPIC (kə-lId-ə-skop′-ik) adj.: continually changing, extremely varied

A KALEIDOSCOPE is a tube that contains mirrors and pieces of colored glass. When the tube is turned, the glass appears in an endless variety of multicolored patterns. The adjective KALEIDOSCOPIC means "formed by or relating to a KALEIDOSCOPE." See *-ic* under Suffixes. The word is usually used in a general sense, about shapes or events that are constantly shifting into new patterns, as if seen through a KALEIDOSCOPE.

"The reporters could barely keep up with the KALEIDOSCOPIC events of the day."

"It was a time of KALEIDOSCOPIC change, when no one knew what to expect next."

Other forms of the word: KALEIDOSCOPE, n.

TORRENT (tor′-ənt or tôr-ənt) n.: a flood, deluge

A TORRENT is a rush or surge of water or other liquid. The word stresses the rapidity and violence of the water.

"Their rowboat was swept away in the TORRENT."

"A TORRENT of lava flooded the city at the foot of the volcano."

TORRENT is also used about any kind of sudden surge.

"The quarterback was greeted with a TORRENT of abuse from the crowd."

PATERNAL (pə-ter′-nəl) adj.: having to do with a father, fatherly

PATERNAL comes from *pater,* the Latin word for *father,* and means "like or of a father." See *-al* under Suffixes.

"He took a PATERNAL interest in the boy. He treated him as if he were his own son."

"I didn't like his PATERNAL attitude. He talked to me like a father talking to his little girl."

Similar words are *maternal,* meaning *motherly,* and *fraternal,* meaning *brotherly.*

ZENITH (zE′-nith) n.: a peak, summit, highest point

In astronomy, the ZENITH is the point in the sky that is directly overhead. ZENITH has come to mean the peak or highest point of anything.

"The singer's popularity reached its ZENITH just after World War II."

"He was at the ZENITH of his powers when he was tragically killed in an auto accident."

"The country's prosperity was at its ZENITH for only a short time before the depression started."

BIGOTED (big'-ət-id) adj.: intolerant, narrow-minded

A BIGOT is a person who is completely intolerant of any belief, opinion, or religion that differs from his own.

> "He is such a BIGOT that he won't even speak to someone who doesn't belong to the same party as he does."

BIGOTED is the adjective from BIGOT.

> "He complained that the company executives were BIGOTED and would hire only people of their own religion."
>
> "They didn't want to appear BIGOTED, so they invited people of different races, creeds, and political parties to the conference."

The most common mistakes for BIGOTED in the Pretest are *vicious* and *greedy*. People who make those mistakes perhaps know that it is bad to be BIGOTED, but don't know exactly why.

Other forms of the word: BIGOT, n.
BIGOTRY, n.

EXCEPTIONAL (ek-sep'-shən-əl) adj.: unusual, rare, uncommon

An EXCEPTION is something that doesn't follow the rule.

> "All the students passed the test with one EXCEPTION—Tommy Jones."

EXCEPTIONAL is the adjective from EXCEPTION. See *-al* under Suffixes. Something that is EXCEPTIONAL is out of the ordinary, doesn't follow the rule.

> "There have been an EXCEPTIONAL number of warm days this spring."

The word is usually used in a positive sense, about something that is better than average or uncommonly good.

> "He thought it was an EXCEPTIONAL movie—one of the best he'd seen."

Most people who make a mistake on this word choose *perfect* as the synonym. Something that is EXCEPTIONAL may be unusually good, but it is not necessarily *perfect*.

Other forms of the word: EXCEPT, v., prep.
EXCEPTION, n.

IMPERATIVE (im-per'-ə-tiv) adj.: urgent, essential, obligatory, pressing

IMPERATIVE is related to the words *emperor* and *imperial*. All come from a Latin word meaning to *command*. Something that is IMPERATIVE is like a command; it is not to be disobeyed or avoided.

> "She said it was IMPERATIVE that we treat the most badly injured soldiers first."
>
> "It is IMPERATIVE that we leave this building before it collapses."

In grammar, an IMPERATIVE sentence is one that expresses a command. "Stop that right now!" is an IMPERATIVE sentence.

PERCEIVE (pər-sEv') v.: to notice, observe, become aware of, sense

To PERCEIVE something is to become aware of it, especially through the senses.

> "We PERCEIVED a faint light in the distance."
>
> "He could PERCEIVE very small differences in sounds."
>
> "The critics failed to PERCEIVE the greatness of the novel until many years later."

Trick is often chosen as the meaning of PERCEIVE. This is probably due to a confusion of PERCEIVE with *deceive*, which means to *trick*.

Other forms of the word: PERCEPTIBLE, adj.
PERCEPTION, n.
PERCEPTIVE, adj.

Exercise 1

Answer each question with a Yes or NO. Put a check in the space for YES or NO next to the question.

		Yes	No
EXAMPLE	Is a speck of dust TINY?	✓	
1.	Do ordinary citizens LEVY taxes?		
2.	Could an ONSLAUGHT be dangerous?		
3.	Do you assist someone by THWARTING him?		
4.	Would a DEGENERATE make a pleasant neighbor?		
5.	Do most people belong to the social ELITE?		
6.	Do people get excited about INDIFFERENT movies?		
7.	Are KALEIDOSCOPIC events often exciting?		
8.	Would your PATERNAL grandfather be your father's father?		
9.	When a person talks about something in RETROSPECT, is he talking about the future?		
10.	Can someone speak with a TORRENT of words?		
11.	If someone's reputation is at its ZENITH, is it as high as it will ever get?		
12.	Does a BIGOT believe that everyone should be treated equally?		
13.	Would it be EXCEPTIONAL for someone to run a mile in less than three minutes?		
14.	Is "Are you coming?" an IMPERATIVE sentence?		
15.	Can you PERCEIVE something with your eyes?		

Exercise 2

Each sentence contains a test word in CAPITAL letters. Decide whether the test word is being used correctly or incorrectly in the sentence. Put a check in the space for RIGHT or WRONG next to the sentence.

		Right	Wrong
EXAMPLE	After working hard all day Bill felt TINY and wanted to sleep.		✓
1.	Congress passed an additional LEVY on imported oil.		
2.	The ONSLAUGHT of the blizzard caught them completely unprepared.		
3.	Every time she tried to go to the beach something happened to THWART her plans.		
4.	The new power plant DEGENERATES a great deal of electricity.		
5.	Several ELITE musicians were chosen to play at the White House.		
6.	The judge was INDIFFERENT to the criminal's cries for mercy.		

		Right	Wrong
7.	The result was completely KALEIDOSCOPIC. All our work was ruined.	______	______
8.	Her PATERNAL instincts were aroused whenever she saw a newborn baby.	______	______
9.	In RETROSPECT we realized we should have paid more attention to our parents.	______	______
10.	The lake was so calm and peaceful it looked like a TORRENT.	______	______
11.	Fads quickly reach the ZENITH of their popularity, and then they fade away just as quickly.	______	______
12.	His BIGOTED attitude makes it difficult for him to accept others on their individual merits.	______	______
13.	The fourth pair of skis was EXCEPTIONAL, since only three of us were going skiing.	______	______
14.	The teacher felt it was IMPERATIVE that her students be able to read well.	______	______
15.	Too late he PERCEIVED that she had been right from the start.	______	______

Exercise 3

Each test word is followed by three other words. Decide which of the three words is LEAST CLOSELY RELATED in its meaning to the meaning of the test word. Put the letter for the word you choose in the space at the end of the line.

EXAMPLE

	TINY:	a) small	b) short	c) angry	C
1.	LEVY:	a) gift	b) tax	c) fine	______
2.	ONSLAUGHT:	a) battle	b) retreat	c) assault	______
3.	THWART:	a) bother	b) frustrate	c) despise	______
4.	DEGENERATE:	a) decay	b) defend	c) decline	______
5.	ELITE:	a) young	b) noble	c) best	______
6.	INDIFFERENT:	a) ridiculous	b) unbiased	c) average	______
7.	KALEIDOSCOPIC:	a) changing	b) improving	c) varying	______
8.	PATERNAL:	a) brotherly	b) fatherly	c) grandfatherly	______
9.	RETROSPECT:	a) memory	b) decision	c) past	______
10.	TORRENT:	a) rapid	b) strength	c) heat	______
11.	ZENITH:	a) top	b) acme	c) beginning	______
12.	BIGOTED:	a) intolerant	b) contemptuous	c) impatient	______
13.	EXCEPTIONAL:	a) pleasant	b) rare	c) outstanding	______
14.	IMPERATIVE:	a) important	b) crucial	c) unusual	______
15.	PERCEIVE:	a) view	b) comprehend	c) select	______

Chapter 2

Pretest

Each test word is printed in CAPITAL letters in a phrase. From the five choices on the next line, select the one which comes nearest in meaning to the meaning of the test word. Underline the one you select.

1. Was it IMPAIRED?
   weakened — increased — destroyed — improved — changed
2. Another SYNOPSIS.
   conclusion — prediction — viewpoint — summary — report
3. Unending BLISS.
   joy — sorrow — excitement — laughter — prayers
4. He INFRINGED the agreement.
   tore up — opposed — hated — wrote — broke
5. Studied the MICROBE.
   atom — star — germ — loudspeaker — spotlight
6. Talked to the NONENTITY.
   masked man — same one — new soldier — clerk — unimportant person
7. TREMULOUS hands.
   tiny — steady — huge — broken — quivering
8. Complete VOID.
   total — change — confusion — emptiness — darkness
9. He ASSAILED it.
   approved — attacked — destroyed — launched — despised
10. His HYPOCRISY.
    vanity — insincerity — theory — interest — hatred
11. DESTITUTE people.
    unhappy — diseased — wealthy — poor — filthy
12. ENDOWED by our Creator.
    provided — loved — taken away — permitted — made
13. IMBECILIC remarks.
    drunken — funny — important — religious — idiotic
14. LOATH to go.
    not ready — eager — unwilling — unable — happy
15. Saw the THRONG.
    boat — shoe — family — crowd — king

IMPAIR (im-pair') v.: to make worse, weaken, injure

To IMPAIR something is to make it worse, to do harm to it. The word often suggests damage that gradually increases.

"Smoking cigarettes will damage your lungs and IMPAIR your breathing."

"His eyesight was IMPAIRED by reading in very dim light."

"The scandal will IMPAIR their chances of winning the election."

In the Pretest, many people choose *destroy* as the meaning of IMPAIR. When you IMPAIR something, you cause it some damage, but you do not *destroy* it.

SYNOPSIS (si-nop'-sis) n.: a summary, outline

A SYNOPSIS is a short summary or outline, usually of the plot of a book, play, or movie.

"It was difficult to make an understandable SYNOPSIS of a book with so many characters doing so many different things."

"According to the SYNOPSIS, the next act takes place in the living room."

"The announcer gave a SYNOPSIS of the president's speech and summarized the main ideas."

"We hurriedly read through several SYNOPSES to prepare for the test."

Usage: The plural form of SYNOPSIS is SYNOPSES.

BLISS (blis) n.: joy, happiness, delight

BLISS is a state of complete happiness or great joy. It is a very strong word, and often refers to the joys of heaven.

"She was unhappy in life, but hoped for eternal BLISS after death."

"When he fell in love, he realized he had never known such BLISS before."

"Their years of perfect BLISS were ended when he became ill."

BLISSFUL is the adjective from BLISS and means "full of or causing great happiness." "BLISSFUL ignorance" is happiness resulting from a lack of knowledge of events or circumstances that could cause unhappiness.

"They lived in BLISSFUL ignorance of the great dangers that surrounded them."

Other forms of the word: BLISSFUL, adj.

INFRINGE (in-frinj') v.: to break, violate; to encroach, trespass

To INFRINGE a rule, law, or agreement is to break it, to fail to obey it.

"He accused us of INFRINGING the contract we had signed with him."

"They INFRINGED the treaty by sending troops into the other country."

INFRINGE is often used with *on* or *upon* to mean "to break in upon," to *encroach.*

"We must never INFRINGE upon the rights of others."

The noun form of INFRINGE is INFRINGEMENT, the act of violating or trespassing.

"He was accused of copyright infringement because he printed the photo in his book without getting the photographer's authorization."

Other forms of the word: INFRINGEMENT, n.

MICROBE (mI'-krOb) n.: a bacterium, germ

The prefix *micro-* means *very small.* It is used in the word *microscope,* which is an instrument that helps you to see very small objects. A MICROBE is a very small living creature, one that is invisible to the naked eye. The word is used especially about small living things that cause diseases.

"There are thousands of tiny MICROBES in the air we breathe."

"The scientists tried to discover the MICROBE that was responsible for the mysterious deaths of the animals."

The most commonly chosen incorrect answer is *atom.* An *atom,* of course, is a very small thing—in fact, far smaller than a MICROBE. The key difference is that a MICROBE is *alive* while an atom isn't.

NONENTITY (non-en'-tə-tE) n.: an unimportant person or thing

An ENTITY is something that exists. The basic meaning of NONENTITY is "something that does not really exist." See *non-* under Prefixes. Usually, though, NONENTITY is used about a person who is so undistinguished and insignificant that it is as if he didn't exist.

"Although he came from a famous family, he himself was a NONENTITY."

"Everyone thought he was a complete NONENTITY, but then it turned out he was a prince in disguise."

TREMULOUS (trem′-yə-ləs) adj.: quivering, trembling; timid, fearful

TREMULOUS is related to the word *tremble.* Someone or something that is TREMULOUS trembles or shakes.

"The old lady could not hold the cup of tea in her TREMULOUS hands."

When used about a person, TREMULOUS sometimes suggests that the trembling is due to fear or nervousness.

"The boy TREMULOUSLY asked the girl if she would dance with him."

Many people pick *huge* as the meaning of TREMULOUS. They are probably confusing TREMULOUS with *tremendous,* which sounds and looks very much like it.

VOID (voyd) n.: emptiness, vacancy

A VOID is an empty, unfilled space.

"He gazed into the limitless VOID of outer space."

"There is an aching VOID in my heart since you left me."

"The car plunged over the cliff and into the VOID."

VOID is also an adjective, meaning *empty, vacant.* The word is usually found in the legal term, "null and VOID," which means "having no legal force."

"The judge declared that the contract was null and VOID."

VOID is also used in this sense as a verb, meaning to *nullify.*

"The judge VOIDED the contract."

ASSAIL (ə-sAl′) v.: to attack, assault

To ASSAIL someone is to attack him, usually suddenly or repeatedly.

"The mob ASSAILED the soldiers with rocks and sticks."

"He was ASSAILED by blows on the head as he tried to escape from the crowd."

ASSAIL can be used in a general sense about any kind of attack.

"As soon as he started the project he was ASSAILED by doubts about whether it would be successful."

An ASSAILANT is someone who attacks.

"Dick was beaten up in the alley by several unknown ASSAILANTS."

Other forms of the word: ASSAILANT, n.

HYPOCRISY (hi-pok′-rə-sE) n.: insincerity, deceit

HYPOCRISY comes from a Greek word meaning *acting.* Someone who practices HYPOCRISY acts good or virtuous when in reality he isn't.

"I can't believe his HYPOCRISY. He always talks about how wrong it is to lie, and he's the worst liar I know."

"The reporter exposed the HYPOCRISY of the religious leader who in private was a cruel and evil man."

A HYPOCRITE is someone who pretends to be virtuous when he isn't.

"They're all HYPOCRITES who don't practice what they preach."

Vanity is a popular choice as the meaning of HYPOCRISY. Both *vanity* and HYPOCRISY are vices, but a person can have one fault without the other.

Other forms of the word: HYPOCRITE, n.
HYPOCRITICAL, adj.

DESTITUTE (des′-tə-tUt) adj.: extremely poor, needy; lacking, deprived

Someone who is DESTITUTE is absolutely penniless and lacks the basic necessities of life, such as food, clothing, and shelter.

"They had always been poor, but the fire left them homeless and completely DESTITUTE."

"I have never been DESTITUTE, but I know what it's like to go hungry."

"When Mr. Jones died, his widow was left DESTITUTE."

The phrase DESTITUTE *of* means *lacking, not having, devoid.*

"We could tell the tree was dying because it was completely DESTITUTE of leaves in the middle of the summer."

"The cruel dictator was DESTITUTE of ordinary human feelings."

ENDOW (en-dow′) v.: to provide, give

ENDOW means to *give* or *provide* something for the benefit of a person or an institution.

"The grateful parent ENDOWED a new wing in the hospital in his son's name."

"The school is looking for someone to ENDOW a new library."

To be ENDOWED *with* something is to have it naturally.

"She is ENDOWED with a great talent for painting."

"He was ENDOWED with the gift for making money."

The noun form of ENDOW is ENDOWMENT, which means a *gift,* usually of money or property.

"Harvard College received an ENDOWMENT of several hundred books."

Other forms of the word: ENDOWMENT, n.

IMBECILIC (im-bə-sil′-ik) adj.: idiotic, weak-minded

An IMBECILE is an extremely weak-minded person, one who cannot develop mentally beyond the age of about seven. IMBECILIC is the adjective from IMBECILE, and means "like an IMBECILE." See *-ic* under Suffixes.

"His actions were so IMBECILIC that no one could believe he was an adult."

"She said Bill's ideas were IMBECILIC and not worth discussing."

Other forms of the word: IMBECILE, n.

LOATH (lOth) adj.: unwilling, reluctant, disinclined

LOATH means *extremely unwilling, reluctant.*

"He was LOATH to go."

"They were LOATH to lend us any more money until we had paid back what we already owed."

"I am LOATH to sign anything I haven't read first."

Do not confuse LOATH and *loathe* (pronounced lOTH). The verb *loathe* means to *hate,* to *despise.*

"I *loathe* having to get up early."

LOATH has a similar meaning, but is only used as an adjective.

"He is LOATH to stay behind. He *loathes* being left out of anything."

Usage: LOATH is also sometimes spelled *loth.*

THRONG (throng) n.: a crowd, multitude

A THRONG is a great number of people crowded together.

"THRONGS of people came to see the hit movie."

"The small child got lost in the THRONG at the parade."

THRONG is also a verb, meaning to *crowd together* or to *fill by crowding.*

"People THRONGED into the street for the parade."

"The park was THRONGED with people waiting to hear the concert."

Exercise 1

Answer each question with a YES or NO. Put a check in the space for YES or NO next to the question.

		Yes	No
EXAMPLE	Is a speck of dust TINY?	✓	
1.	Will eating poisoned food IMPAIR your health?		
2.	Does the SYNOPSIS of a book include every word?		
3.	Is BLISS a pleasant sensation?		
4.	Would most people like to have somebody INFRINGE upon their rights?		
5.	Is it difficult to see a MICROBE?		
6.	Was Julius Caesar a NONENTITY?		
7.	Would TREMULOUS handwriting be difficult to read?		
8.	Can a VOID be very large?		
9.	Do people enjoy being ASSAILED?		
10.	Are HYPOCRITES usually trustworthy?		
11.	Would a millionaire be DESTITUTE?		
12.	Are pigs ENDOWED with the ability to fly?		
13.	Would most people like to be called IMBECILIC?		
14.	Are children usually LOATH to eat ice cream?		
15.	Are you a THRONG?		

Exercise 2

Each sentence contains a test word in CAPITAL letters. Decide whether the test word is being used correctly or incorrectly in the sentence. Put a check in the space for RIGHT or WRONG next to the sentence.

		Right	Wrong
EXAMPLE	After working hard all day Bill felt TINY and wanted to sleep.		✓
1.	He IMPAIRED the two of us and decided I was the better.		
2.	After reading the SYNOPSIS of the TV show in the newspaper, we decided not to watch it.		
3.	Their BLISSFUL marriage lasted over fifty years.		
4.	The truce between the countries was INFRINGED when enemy soldiers attacked our town.		
5.	The doctor examined the tissue under the microscope to try to spot the MICROBES.		
6.	The public relations man said he could take any NONENTITY and make him world famous in six weeks.		

		Right	Wrong
7.	In a TREMULOUS voice he said he'd never been so scared in his entire life.	✓	
8.	We built the biggest VOID in the city.		✓
9.	Police searched for the ASSAILANT who had attacked the man in broad daylight.	✓	
10.	She felt it was HYPOCRISY to say you liked a person if you really didn't.	✓	
11.	This program is terrible. The actors on it are completely DESTITUTE of talent.	✓	
12.	We are ENDOWED with certain rights under our Constitution.	✓	
13.	Everyone praised the play as being truly IMBECILIC.		✓
14.	The boss was LOATH to fire anyone just before Christmas.	✓	
15.	THRONGS of people visited the museum for the display of Egyptian treasures.	✓	

Exercise 3

Each test word is followed by three other words. Decide which of the three words is LEAST CLOSELY RELATED in its meaning to the meaning of the test word. Put the letter for the word you choose in the space at the end of the line.

EXAMPLE

	TINY:	a) small	b) short	c) angry	C
1.	IMPAIR:	a) harm	b) force	c) damage	B
2.	SYNOPSIS :	a) addition	b) outline	c) sketch	A
3.	BLISS:	a) excitement	b) happiness	c) delight	A
4.	INFRINGE:	a) violate	b) forget	c) trespass	B
5.	MICROBE:	a) tininess	b) creature	c) brightness	C
6.	NONENTITY:	a) unknown	b) being	c) insignificance	B
7.	TREMULOUS:	a) shaking	b) afraid	c) nasty	C
8.	VOID:	a) distant	b) hollow	c) vacant	A
9.	ASSAIL:	a) hit	b) beat	c) chase	C
10.	HYPOCRISY:	a) lie	b) pretense	c) argument	C
11.	DESTITUTE:	a) starving	b) penniless	c) forgotten	C
12.	ENDOW:	a) give	b) finance	c) insure	C
13.	IMBECILIC:	a) idiotic	b) silly	c) humorous	C
14.	LOATH:	a) required	b) opposed	c) hesitant	A
15.	THRONG:	a) battle	b) horde	c) mob	A

Chapter 3

Pretest

Each test word is printed in CAPITAL letters in a phrase. From the five choices on the next line, select the one which comes nearest in meaning to the meaning of the test word. Underline the one you select.

1.	Watched them CAVORT.				
	rest	make merry	eat	answer	change
2.	He will CONCEDE it.				
	overcome	announce	deny	admit	lose
3.	INTEGRAL parts.				
	different	reliable	essential	useless	perfect
4.	DOTING parents.				
	capable	overly fond	mean-spirited	cheerful	self-satisfied
5.	INTERIM chief.				
	next	new	first	temporary	former
6.	LACKLUSTER performances.				
	pleasant	overwhelming	terrible	dull	sad
7.	Sudden CONVULSION.				
	hope	hatred	urge	fit	illness
8.	PLAUSIBLE excuse.				
	unusual	typical	perfect	poor	likely
9.	WHIMSICAL ideas.				
	playful	serious	original	useless	dangerous
10.	More ABORIGINES.				
	slaves	natives	mountains	foreigners	animals
11.	CEREBRAL activity.				
	happy	mental	physical	religious	serious
12.	To INCITE the rebellion.				
	understand	stir up	put down	plan	approve of
13.	COSMOPOLITAN interests.				
	expensive	immoral	religious	local	worldwide
14.	We knew its DERIVATION.				
	source	purpose	contents	meaning	result
15.	Ended the FRACAS.				
	game	silence	party	fight	meeting

CAVORT (kə-vôrt′) v.: to make merry, prance, jump about

To CAVORT is to make merry, usually by jumping and dancing about. The word was originally used about a horse and its rider.

"The mother dog looked on calmly while her puppies CAVORTED in the tall grass."

"We enjoyed watching the children CAVORTING on the beach."

"The students CAVORTED on the steps of the school, happy to be going home at last."

CONCEDE (kən-sEd′) v.: to admit, acknowledge; to grant, surrender

CONCEDE has two different meanings. To CONCEDE something is to admit that it is true.

"After a long debate Ed finally CONCEDED the point and said we were right."

"We CONCEDED that we had been a bit hasty in criticizing her."

The word can also mean to *grant* or *surrender*.

"When Jim injured his foot he had to CONCEDE the match to his opponent."

"As part of the peace treaty they CONCEDED all the territory they had won in the war."

The most common mistake in the Pretest is to choose *deny* as the meaning of CONCEDE. This is a confusion of a word with its opposite. People who choose *deny* as the meaning of CONCEDE perhaps know that CONCEDE has something to do with the truth, but aren't exactly sure what.

Other forms of the word: CONCESSION, n.

INTEGRAL (in′-tə-grəl or in-teg′-rəl) adj.: necessary for completeness, essential

INTEGRAL is from a Latin word meaning *whole, entire,* also the source of the word *integer.* An *integer,* in arithmetic, is a whole number (1, 2, 3, 4, . . .) as opposed to a fraction. Something that is INTEGRAL to something else is necessary for its completeness.

"This piece is INTEGRAL to the machine. If you remove it, nothing will work."

INTEGRAL is often found in the phrase "an INTEGRAL part of," which means a *necessary* or *essential* part of.

"Learning vocabulary is an INTEGRAL part of education; without words you can't read."

DOTING (dOt′-ing) adj.: overly fond; weak-minded

To DOTE on someone is to show excessive affection for him.

"Our grandmother DOTES on us; she'll give us anything we want."

DOTING is the adjective from DOTE, and means "showing too much fondness."

"The DOTING parents couldn't keep their eyes off their new baby."

"The DOTING husband brought his wife flowers every night."

In another sense, DOTING is sometimes used to mean *weak-minded,* especially from old age. This sense is particularly found in the noun DOTAGE, which means "feebleness of mind resulting from old age."

"In his DOTAGE his mind started to wander and it was hard to understand him."

Other forms of the word: DOTAGE, n.
DOTE, v.

INTERIM (in′-tər-im) adj.: temporary, provisional

INTERIM comes directly from a Latin word which means "in the meantime," *meanwhile.* INTERIM is used as a noun in the phrase "in the INTERIM," which means exactly the same as the Latin word. As an adjective, INTERIM means "done or occurring in the meantime," *temporary.*

"They issued an INTERIM report until the new set of figures came in and they could make it final."

"They set up an INTERIM government to rule while the new constitution was being written."

LACKLUSTER (lak′-luhs-tər) adj.: dull, uninspired

Luster is *brightness,* the glow of a polished surface. Something which is LACKLUSTER lacks *luster* or brightness; it is dull, uninspired. The word is especially used about expressions, actions, events, and the like.

"She always had a LACKLUSTER expression on her face, as if she weren't interested in anything."

"It was a LACKLUSTER performance—nothing very good about it, nothing very bad about it."

Many people think LACKLUSTER means *terrible.* LACKLUSTER, however, is not that strong. It merely means *dull, uninteresting, lacking brilliance.*

CONVULSION (kən-vuhl′-shən) n.: a fit, disturbance, upheaval

To CONVULSE is to shake violently.

"California was CONVULSED by an earthquake."

CONVULSION is the noun from CONVULSE. A CONVULSION is a violent shaking or disturbance, particularly the uncontrolled irregular movements of the muscles during a fit. In this case the word is usually used in the plural.

"The child went into CONVULSIONS after she swallowed the poison."

A CONVULSION can also be any kind of disturbance or upheaval.

"Constant social CONVULSIONS kept the nation in a state of chaos for years."

The most popular wrong answers on the Pretest are *illness* and *urge.* A CONVULSION can be caused by an *illness,* but its meaning is much more specific. The choice of *urge* is probably due in most cases to a confusion between CONVULSION and *compulsion,* which is a strong *urge.*

Other forms of the word: CONVULSE, v.
CONVULSIVE, adj.

PLAUSIBLE (plô′-zə-bəl) adj.: likely, apparently reasonable

Something that is PLAUSIBLE has the appearance of being true. A PLAUSIBLE argument sounds true and makes sense, even if in fact it is not true.

"He gave the teacher a PLAUSIBLE reason about why he hadn't done his homework."

"Her excuse sounded PLAUSIBLE at the time, but later on we found out she had been lying."

The opposite of PLAUSIBLE is IMPLAUSIBLE, which mean *unlikely, improbable.*

"The account of his adventures sounded IMPLAUSIBLE, but in fact that was exactly what had happened."

Other forms of the word: PLAUSIBILITY, n.

WHIMSICAL (hwim′-zə-kəl or wim′-zə-kəl) adj.: playful, fanciful, fantastic

WHIMSICAL is an adjective from WHIMSY. See *-ic* under Suffixes. WHIMSY is odd or fanciful humor, or the product of such humor.

"He is full of WHIMSY; he always has such fanciful ideas."

Someone or something that is WHIMSICAL is full of such odd notions or behavior.

"Although usually very serious, he could sometimes be very strange and WHIMSICAL."

"Her WHIMSICAL behavior bewildered everyone. She was always doing the oddest things at the most unexpected times."

"He told the children a WHIMSICAL story about how elves paint the grass green."

Other forms of the word: WHIM, n.
WHIMSY, n.

ABORIGINE (ab-ə-rij′-ə-nE) n.: a native, original inhabitant

Note the pronunciation. The *e* is sounded.

You can see the word *origin* in ABORIGINE. ABORIGINE comes from the Latin phrase *ab origine,* which means "from the beginning." An ABORIGINE is one of the native people of a region or country. ABORIGINES have lived in a particular region "from the beginning." They were the very first people to come into the region from somewhere else and settle there.

"The colonists arriving from across the sea found the ABORIGINES friendly and willing to share their land."

"The invading tribe conquered the ABORIGINES and made them leave their native land."

The word ABORIGINES is also used for the original flowers and animals in a particular region.

Other forms of the word: ABORIGINAL, adj.

CEREBRAL (ser′-ə-brəl or sə-rE′-brəl) adj.: mental, intellectual

The CEREBRUM is a part of the brain. The basic meaning of CEREBRAL is "of the CEREBRUM or the brain." See *-al* under Suffixes. CEREBRAL *palsy* is a disability caused by damage to the brain. When used about people or their activities, CEREBRAL means *intellectual,* as opposed to *emotional.* A CEREBRAL person mainly uses his reasoning and critical powers, and not his intuitions or instincts.

"He is a CEREBRAL writer; his stories aren't exciting, but they give a lot of food for thought."

INCITE (in-sIt′) v.: to stir up, spur on, urge on, arouse

To INCITE is to stir up, to urge somebody to do something. Usually the word suggests that something bad is being stirred up.

"Her fiery speeches INCITED them to riot."

"His tales of gold hidden inside INCITED the crowd to break into the building and steal everything they could find."

"The assassination of the prince INCITED violence between the two warring parties."

The noun from INCITE is INCITEMENT, something that stirs people up.

"The umpire's one bad call was enough of an INCITEMENT for the crowd to boo him for the rest of the game."

Other forms of the word: INCITEMENT, n.

COSMOPOLITAN (koz-mə-pol′-ə-tən) adj.: worldwide, universal, worldly

COSMOPOLITAN comes from two Greek words. The *cosmo* part of the word means *world* or *universe;* it is also found in the words COSMOS and COSMONAUT. The *polit* part means *citizen;* it also appears in *politics* and *police.* COSMOPOLITAN is used about people or things that are at home all over the world. It is especially applied to people who are free from local prejudices or interests, who have a broad, sophisticated outlook.

"Jim has a COSMOPOLITAN background; he lived in six different countries before he was twelve."

"He believed that statesmen should have a COSMOPOLITAN point of view when trying to solve world problems."

DERIVATION (der-ə-vA′-shən) n.: source, origin

To DERIVE means to *take* or *obtain,* especially from a source.

"We DERIVE great pleasure from watching television."

"The name of this town is DERIVED from an Indian word."

The DERIVATION of something is its source or origin.

"What is the DERIVATION of the custom of collecting candy on Halloween?"

DERIVATION is used especially about the development of a word from earlier words.

"Many English words are of Latin DERIVATION."

"The teacher explained the DERIVATION of the word *amateur.*"

Other forms of the word: DERIVATIVE, adj.
DERIVE, v.

FRACAS (frA′-kəs or fra′-kəs) n.: a disturbance, uproar, noisy quarrel, fight, brawl

A FRACAS is a noisy disturbance, an uproar. The word is generally used about people fighting or disagreeing with one another.

"A FRACAS erupted among some spectators who had been drinking."

"Two policemen were injured trying to end the FRACAS."

"A nice party suddenly became a FRACAS when everyone started arguing about politics."

A FRACAS is smaller and less serious than a *riot,* but larger and usually more violent than a *quarrel.*

Exercise 1

Answer each question with a YES or NO. Put a check in the space for YES or NO next to the question.

	Yes	No
EXAMPLE Is a speck of dust TINY?	✓	
1. Do snakes usually CAVORT?		
2. Would a stubborn person enjoy CONCEDING something?		
3. Is the engine an INTEGRAL part of a car?		
4. Would a DOTING father be proud of his children?		
5. Will an INTERIM plan always be used?		
6. Would a LACKLUSTER game be very exciting?		
7. Are CONVULSIONS usually pleasant?		
8. Can PLAUSIBLE explanations be false?		
9. Could a WHIMSICAL story be amusing?		
10. Were the Pilgrims ABORIGINES in America?		
11. Is falling in love a CEREBRAL activity?		
12. Would a raise in pay sometimes INCITE people to work harder?		
13. Would a COSMOPOLITAN newspaper contain just local news?		
14. Do names have DERIVATIONS?		
15. Could people get hurt in a FRACAS?		

Exercise 2

Each sentence contains a test word in CAPITAL letters. Decide whether the test word is being used correctly or incorrectly in the sentence. Put a check in the space for RIGHT or WRONG next to the sentence.

	Right	Wrong
EXAMPLE After working hard all day Bill felt TINY and wanted to sleep.		✓
1. We were so excited we CAVORTED through the halls of the school.		
2. It was certain that he was going to lose, but he refused to CONCEDE defeat.		
3. The idea that there was intelligent life on other planets was INTEGRAL to his theory about the universe.		
4. The DOTING boy stopped six different places on his way home from school.		
5. This is just an INTERIM solution to the problem; we'll have to come up with something better before long.		
6. Her dancing is brilliant, but her singing is LACKLUSTER.		
7. The comedian's jokes CONVULSED us with laughter; we laughed so hard our sides were aching.		

		Right	Wrong
8.	He told an IMPLAUSIBLE tale about a trip he took to Mars.	____	____
9.	We heard a WHIMSICAL story about bloodshed, torture, and death.	____	____
10.	The ABORIGINES could not defend their island against the invaders.	____	____
11.	He suffered a CEREBRAL in his leg.	____	____
12.	The general INCITED the private for outstanding bravery.	____	____
13.	Her COSMOPOLITAN interests took her to Europe at least once a year.	____	____
14.	She DERIVED a great deal of satisfaction from seeing her son graduate from college.	____	____
15.	I was afraid the meeting would turn into a FRACAS if people lost their tempers.	____	____

Exercise 3

Each test word is followed by three other words. Decide which of the three words is LEAST CLOSELY RELATED in its meaning to the meaning of the test word. Put the letter for the word you choose in the space at the end of the line.

EXAMPLE

	TINY:	a) small	b) short	c) angry	C
1.	CAVORT:	a) dance	b) climb	c) jump	____
2.	CONCEDE:	a) yield	b) grant	c) dispute	____
3.	INTEGRAL:	a) whole	b) helpful	c) necessary	____
4.	DOTING:	a) recognizable	b) fond	c) loving	____
5.	INTERIM:	a) unusual	b) provisional	c) temporary	____
6.	LACKLUSTER:	a) average	b) boring	c) harmful	____
7.	CONVULSION:	a) trembling	b) fear	c) turbulence	____
8.	PLAUSIBLE:	a) reasonable	b) probable	c) certain	____
9.	WHIMSICAL:	a) scary	b) odd	c) silly	____
10.	ABORIGINE:	a) original	b) native	c) despot	____
11.	CEREBRAL:	a) desirable	b) brainy	c) thoughtful	____
12.	INCITE:	a) spur	b) defend	c) encourage	____
13.	COSMOPOLITAN:	a) worldly	b) sophisticated	c) young	____
14.	DERIVATION:	a) outcome	b) source	c) origin	____
15.	FRACAS:	a) riot	b) brawl	c) conversation	____

Review Test 1—Chapters 1–3

Fill in each blank with the test word (or a form of the test word) which best fits the sentence. Use the words listed below.

ABORIGINE	CONVULSION	ELITE	INDIFFERENT	NONENTITY
ASSAIL	DEGENERATE	FRACAS	INFRINGE	PLAUSIBLE
BIGOT	DESTITUTE	HYPOCRISY	INTEGRAL	THRONG
CEREBRAL	DOTING	IMBECILIC	LOATH	TORRENT
CONCEDE				

1. We found out about his ___HYPOCRISY___ when he told us how important it was not to lose your temper. He has the worst temper I've ever seen.
2. He was a member of the educational ___ELITE___ —one of the greatest professors in the country.
3. The party began very pleasantly, but by midnight it had ___DEGENERATE___ into a drunken brawl.
4. He had the ___IMBECILIC___ notion that if he flapped his arms fast enough he would be able to fly.
5. Since she was taught from childhood to hate and fear those who were of a different race, it was only natural for her to be ___BIGOT___.
6. The illness caused him to go into sudden ___CONVULSION___ during which he lost control of his muscles.
7. The dog gets very upset if another animal ___INFRINGE___ on her territory.
8. The ___DOTING___ grandparents showed pictures of the new baby to all their friends.
9. Jack was ___LOATH___ to go to college if it meant leaving behind all his friends.
10. When the dam burst, a(n) ___TORRENT___ of water gushed out and flooded the valley.
11. The enemy ___ASSAIL___ our position with a hail of gunfire and bombs.
12. Linda was ___INDIFFERENT___ to John's difficulties; she didn't care if he solved his problems.
13. When we pressed him about it, he ___CONCEDE___ that he did sometimes lose his temper.
14. While he was alive, people thought that he was a complete ___NONENTITY___, but after he died they realized what a great artist he had been.
15. There was a(n) ___FRACAS___ outside the theater as people started pushing and shoving to get in.
16. Playing chess is a(n) ___CEREBRAL___ activity; you really have to use your mind to do it well.
17. A(n) ___THRONG___ of eager fans jammed into the airport to see the movie star.
18. When the explorers reached the valley, they found a tribe of ___ABORIGINE___ who must have lived there for thousands of years.
19. When our father lost his job we were ___DESTITUTE___; we didn't even have enough money to buy food.
20. The coach told Ed he was a(n) ___INTEGRAL___ part of the team. He said they couldn't get along without him.
21. Jim's explanation sounded ___PLAUSIBLE___, but I still didn't believe him.

Fill in each blank with the test word (or a form of the test word) which best fits the sentence. Use the words listed below.

BLISS	EXCEPTIONAL	KALEIDOSCOPIC	PATERNAL	TREMULOUS
CAVORT	IMPAIR	LACKLUSTER	PERCEIVE	VOID
COSMOPOLITAN	IMPERATIVE	LEVY	RETROSPECT	WHIMSICAL
DERIVATION	INCITE	MICROBE	SYNOPSIS	ZENITH
ENDOW	INTERIM	ONSLAUGHT	THWART	

22. He was unable to ____________ the difference between the two colors.

23. The millionaire promised to ____________ a stadium for the school if they would name it after him.

24. They reached a(n) ____________ agreement that would last until they could settle the dispute once and for all.

25. His fiery words so ____________ the crowd that they attacked the police station.

26. When the nation was at the ____________ of its power it ruled over half the world.

27. The ____________ contained a brief summary of the plot and mentioned the main characters.

28. A good dictionary will give both the meaning of a word and its ____________ so that you can see how the word came to us from other languages.

29. The foot injury ____________ his ability to run quickly.

30. He had ____________ skill in playing the piano. Only a few were as good as he was.

31. We knew the enemy was coming, but we were still unable to resist their ____________.

32. The happy children laughed and ____________ in the yard.

33. Nothing could spoil the perfect ____________ of their happy family life.

34. In ____________ it is easy to see how foolish we must have looked to other people.

35. The teacher had a(n) ____________ feeling toward his students. He liked to think of them as his own children.

36. The state ____________ a tax on cigarettes and other tobacco products.

37. She told the children a(n) ____________ story about the adventures of a family of rabbits.

38. It was a(n) ____________ party; nothing very interesting or exciting happened the whole evening.

39. With his ____________ hands he was unable to get the key into the lock.

40. The ____________ changes of this decade make it difficult for a historian to discuss it briefly.

41. The disappearance of her favorite cat left an aching ____________ in her heart.

42. We're looking for someone with a(n) ____________ background: someone who has traveled widely and seen the world.

43. Nothing they could do could ____________ the evil scientist's plan to take over the world.

44. The scientists discovered that a tiny ____________ was causing the terrible disease.

45. The hurricane will hit us any minute; it is ____________ that we seek shelter immediately.

Chapter 4

Pretest

Each test word is printed in CAPITAL letters in a phrase. From the five choices on the next line, select the one which comes nearest in meaning to the meaning of the test word. Underline the one you select.

1. MANIFOLD attractions.
   few | numerous | different | wonderful | obvious
2. Obvious QUIRK.
   intelligence | problem | peculiarity | grin | nervousness
3. The performance was NONPAREIL.
   well-received | unfortunate | unequaled | sloppy | free
4. Unexpected PANGS.
   terrors | expressions | pains | delights | noises
5. Made them SWOON.
   fall | sing | cry | wake up | faint
6. HALLOWED places.
   holy | awful | lovely | ancient | haunted
7. They IMPLORED us.
   told | asked | begged | needed | hated
8. To PROCURE it.
   pay for | protect | obtain | reach | save
9. His ALLOTTED share.
   expected | assigned | permitted | huge | stolen
10. To BLASPHEME them.
    hate | punish | curse | bless | envy
11. During the MELEE.
    rush hour | free-for-all | ambush | quiet evening | war
12. To PLACATE them.
    love | show | ask | arouse | soothe
13. VEHEMENT speech.
    long | difficult | quiet | intense | well-meaning
14. STEADFAST people.
    quick | likable | dangerous | loyal | powerful
15. He seemed ALOOF.
    friendly | lazy | odd | cruel | distant

MANIFOLD (man′-ə-fOld) adj.: numerous, various, diverse

The suffix *-fold* means "multiplied by." To increase something a *hundredfold* means to increase it a hundred times. The *mani-* part of MANIFOLD is the word *many.* So MANIFOLD basically means "multiplied by many." The word is used about things or actions that are numerous and varied, or that have many different features or uses.

"As head of the organization he has MANIFOLD responsibilities."

"One of the machine's MANIFOLD advantages is that it is easy to fix."

The most commonly chosen incorrect answer in the Pretest is *obvious.* This is probably due to a confusion of MANIFOLD with *manifest. Manifest* means "clear to the senses," *evident, obvious.*

QUIRK (kwerk) n.: a peculiarity of behavior

The basic meaning of QUIRK is "a sudden twist or curve." It is still used this way in the phrase "a QUIRK of fate," which is a sudden twist or change of fate. Usually today the word means "twists" of behavior—that is, personal peculiarities or mannerisms.

"If you ignore some of the QUIRKS of his personality, he's really a very nice fellow."

"She has this odd QUIRK of always wanting to be the last one to arrive at a party."

NONPAREIL (non-pə-rel′) adj.: unequaled, having no equal, the best, peerless

NONPAREIL is a French word used in English; it means *not equaled.* See *non-* under Prefixes. Anything which is NONPAREIL cannot be topped. It is the best.

"She has a marvelous, NONPAREIL beauty."

"He was a NONPAREIL boxer."

Sometimes NONPAREIL comes after the word it modifies.

"He was a boxer NONPAREIL."

NONPAREIL is also a noun, meaning "a person or thing that has no equal."

"She was a NONPAREIL as a pianist. I've never heard anyone better."

PANG (pang) n.: a sharp pain

A PANG is a sudden, brief, sharp pain.

"The starving man felt PANGS of hunger."

The word is more commonly used about mental pain than physical pain. It is used about a piercing feeling of sorrow, longing, or a similar strong emotion.

"He suffered PANGS of conscience after he stole the bicycle."

"Jane felt a PANG of envy when she saw how popular Mary was."

"With a PANG of regret they looked back for the last time at their old house."

"She was eighteen when she first felt the PANGS of love."

SWOON (swUn) v.: to faint; to become enraptured.

SWOON means to *faint* or *lose consciousness.* Often SWOON is used about people in a state of sudden excitement or rapture.

"The young girls SWOONED when they saw their favorite singer come into the room."

"He felt faint and nearly SWOONED at the sight of so much beauty."

SWOON is also a noun meaning a *faint* or a *fainting fit.*

"She started to regain consciousness and come out of the SWOON."

HALLOWED (hal′-Od) adj.: holy, sacred, blessed

To HALLOW something is to make it holy or to treat it as sacred. HALLOWED is the adjective from HALLOW and means *sacred, holy.*

"We walked solemnly past the HALLOWED ground of the graveyard."

"No one was allowed to touch the HALLOWED objects that had once belonged to the saint."

November 1 is the Feast of All Saints, which used to be *All* HALLOW. So October 31 is HALLOWEEN, which is short for *All* HALLOW *Evening.*

The most popular mistake on the pretest for HALLOWED is *haunted,* due to the confusion caused by HALLOWEEN and the tales of ghosts and demons we associate with it.

Other forms of the word: HALLOW, v.

IMPLORE (im-plôr') v.: beg, beseech, request earnestly

To IMPLORE someone is to call upon him urgently for help, mercy, or the like.

"I IMPLORE you not to let us down when we need you the most."

"We IMPLORED the teacher not to give us any homework."

To IMPLORE something is to ask for it urgently.

"We IMPLORED his forgiveness."

"He IMPLORED her to help him, and finally she agreed."

IMPLORE means almost exactly the same as *beg,* except that usually IMPLORE is a stronger word.

"I asked him to come. Then I begged him. Finally I IMPLORED him to come."

PROCURE (prO-KyUr' or prə-kyUr') v.: to get, obtain

PROCURE means to *get,* especially as the result of effort and planning.

"We managed to PROCURE our supplies before they ran out."

"She was unable to PROCURE the necessary funds."

"He had to go to a hardware store ten miles away to PROCURE the special tool he wanted."

Protect and *save* are often mistakenly chosen as the meaning of PROCURE, perhaps because of confusion with the word *secure.*

ALLOT (ə-lot') v.: to assign, distribute by lot

Lots are objects like straws or pebbles used to decide something by chance. To *draw lots,* for example, is to choose pieces of paper or the like to decide who will do something, who wins something, etc. To ALLOT something is to distribute it or divide it up as if by lot. Usually the word doesn't suggest the actual drawing of lots.

"He took whatever he was ALLOTTED and didn't complain, even if it was much less than everyone else received."

"The ALLOTTED time for his speech had ended, but he refused to stop talking."

The noun from ALLOT is ALLOTMENT, which means "a share or portion."

"His ALLOTMENT was only nine dollars."

Permit is often thought to be the meaning of ALLOT, probably because ALLOT looks so much like *allow.*

Other forms of the word: ALLOTMENT, n.

BLASPHEME (blas-fEm') v.: to curse, speak irreverently

BLASPHEME comes from a Greek word meaning to *speak evil.* In English BLASPHEME also means to *speak evil,* especially to talk in an irreverent or abusive way about God or something sacred.

"The church leaders said he had BLASPHEMED the name of God by his criticisms of religion."

BLASPHEMY is an act of irreverence toward something sacred.

"The priest said the youths committed BLASPHEMY by writing swear words on the church doors."

Other forms of the word: BLASPHEMOUS, adj.
BLASPHEMY, n.

MELEE (mA'-lA) n.: a confused struggle, free-for-all, brawl

Note the pronunciation. MELEE is a French word, and has kept its French pronunciation.

A MELEE is a confused struggle involving a crowd of people.

"A MELEE broke out among the fans at the football game."

"The police had to use tear gas to break up the MELEE."

MELEE is also used about a confused or disorganized crowd in general, without the suggestion of fighting.

"He elbowed his way through the MELEE of people trying to finish their Christmas shopping."

PLACATE (plA'-kAt) v.: to soothe, pacify, appease, mollify

To PLACATE means to *soothe* someone who is hostile or offended, usually by making concessions.

"In order to PLACATE his teacher Bob did extra homework that weekend."

"We tried to PLACATE Jane, but everything we did seemed to make her even angrier."

"He PLACATED the store owner by agreeing to return everything he had stolen."

VEHEMENT (vE′-ə-mənt) adj.: intense, strong, passionate, emphatic

VEHEMENT means *intense, passionate, earnest.*

> "The lawyer had some VEHEMENT objections to the judge's rulings."

VEHEMENT is often used about the way people talk or act.

> "His VEHEMENT tone left no doubt that he was quite upset about the matter."
>
> "Jim VEHEMENTLY denied having taken the money."

Other forms of the word: VEHEMENCE, n.

STEADFAST (sted′-fast) adj.: faithful, loyal, firm, unswerving

The *stead* part of STEADFAST comes from an old English word meaning *place.* A *homestead,* for example, is a place where you have your home. The *fast* part does not mean *quick* or *speedy*, but comes from another use of the word which means *firmly fixed.* You can see this use of *fast* in the word *fasten.* So something which is STEADFAST is firmly fixed in place. Usually today STEADFAST is used about people, and means "firmly fixed in one's beliefs or loyalties," *faithful, resolute.*

> "He was a STEADFAST friend. He would always help you when you needed it most."
>
> "She STEADFASTLY maintained her innocence despite all the proof that she was guilty."

ALOOF (ə-lUf′) adj.: distant, indifferent, remote

ALOOF is used about people who like to keep the feelings and opinions of others at a distance. ALOOF people stand apart and don't become involved in the affairs of others. Often the word suggests that this happens because these people feel superior to the rest of us.

> "Mary always remained ALOOF from the other children, as if she thought their games were too silly for her."
>
> "He was very warm and friendly with his family, but at work he seemed quite ALOOF."

Exercise 1

Answer each question with a YES or NO. Put a check in the space for YES or NO next to the question.

EXAMPLE

	Yes	No
Is a speck of dust TINY?	✓	
1. Would most people want to buy a house that has MANIFOLD problems?		
2. Is a QUIRK always a bad thing?		
3. Would a NONPAREIL dancer be better than average?		
4. Are PANGS usually pleasant?		
5. Is a person in a SWOON fully awake?		
6. Would a church contain HALLOWED objects?		
7. Would a person who is drowning IMPLORE someone to save him?		
8. Do you have to go to a doctor to PROCURE a disease?		
9. Can food be ALLOTTED?		
10. Is it BLASPHEMY to rob a bank?		
11. Is a MELEE generally peaceful?		
12. Does an angry person like to PLACATE people?		
13. Could a VEHEMENT tone indicate that a person is upset?		
14. Would a STEADFAST friend desert you in time of trouble?		
15. Are salesmen usually ALOOF?		

Exercise 2

Each sentence contains a test word in CAPITAL letters. Decide whether the test word is being used correctly or incorrectly in the sentence. Put a check in the space for RIGHT or WRONG next to the sentence.

EXAMPLE

	Right	Wrong
After working hard all day Bill felt TINY and wanted to sleep.		✓
1. We went to see the MANIFOLD attractions and displays in the museum.		
2. We were so accustomed to his QUIRKS that we were surprised when other people commented on how odd he was.		
3. He was a singer NONPAREIL—perhaps the greatest that ever lived.		
4. He felt a few PANGS of fear as he walked into the haunted house.		
5. She SWOONED with joy when the rock 'n' roll star threw her a flower.		
6. Seeing the ghost really HALLOWED them.		
7. The king IMPLORED them to join the fight against their common enemy.		

		Right	Wrong
8.	We had to PROCURE a license before we were allowed to stay at the camp-grounds.	✓	
9.	The teacher ALLOTTED us each five minutes to speak to the class.	✓	
10.	He BLASPHEMED all religions, calling them the work of the devil.	✓	
11.	Each afternoon there was a MELEE at the bus stop as all the school children tried to get on at once.	✓	
12.	The king refused to do anything to PLACATE the angry mob.	✓	
13.	The leaf drifted VEHEMENTLY down to the ground.		✓
14.	The STEADFAST horse raced around the track in record time.		✓
15.	The rich boy kept ALOOF from all the other children at school.	✓	

Exercise 3

Each test word is followed by three other words. Decide which of the three words is LEAST CLOSELY RELATED in its meaning to the meaning of the test word. Put the letter for the word you choose in the space at the end of the line.

EXAMPLE

	TINY:	**a)** small	**b)** short	**c)** angry	C
1.	MANIFOLD:	**a)** many	**b)** complicated	**c)** varied	B
2.	QUIRK:	**a)** oddity	**b)** strangeness	**c)** pleasantness	C
3.	NONPAREIL:	**a)** good	**b)** marvelous	**c)** perfect	A
4.	PANG:	**a)** ache	**b)** noise	**c)** sorrow	B
5.	SWOON:	**a)** fainting	**b)** unconscious	**c)** sleepy	C
6.	HALLOWED:	**a)** sacred	**b)** beautiful	**c)** divine	B
7.	IMPLORE:	**a)** plead	**b)** beg	**c)** need	C
8.	PROCURE:	**a)** get	**b)** show	**c)** buy	B
9.	ALLOT:	**a)** divide	**b)** distribute	**c)** desire	C
10.	BLASPHEME:	**a)** insult	**b)** refuse	**c)** swear	B
11.	MELEE:	**a)** joy	**b)** crowd	**c)** struggle	A
12.	PLACATE:	**a)** trick	**b)** please	**c)** calm	A
13.	VEHEMENT:	**a)** passionate	**b)** enthusiastic	**c)** vain	C
14.	STEADFAST:	**a)** generous	**b)** faithful	**c)** firm	A
15.	ALOOF:	**a)** talkative	**b)** superior	**c)** indifferent	A

Chapter 5

Pretest

Each test word is printed in CAPITAL letters in a phrase. From the five choices on the next line, select the one which comes nearest in meaning to the meaning of the test word. Underline the one you select.

1. The BENEVOLENT woman.
   lucky — wealthy — kindly — holy — cruel
2. The GUISE of friendship.
   promise — appearance — reality — beauty — hope
3. To CONTRIVE a system.
   learn — consider — improve — invent — oppose
4. How did they DEPICT him?
   like — see — lose — choose — describe
5. JAUNDICED appearance.
   healthy — saddened — yellowish — grayish — frightened
6. She looks PENSIVE.
   nervous — thoughtful — happy — angry — wealthy
7. He SQUANDERS his money.
   misplaces — saves — wastes — worries about — hides
8. ULTERIOR motives.
   pressing — worse — obvious — hidden — dishonest
9. AMASS a treasure.
   give away — find — lose — gather — pray for
10. KINDRED tribes.
    related — happy — friendly — far-off — local
11. New ORDINANCES.
    customs — morals — orders — sheriffs — privileges
12. Reached the KNOLL.
    rock — small hill — cave — top — valley
13. Examined the ORIFICE.
    cave — tunnel — wall — tooth — opening
14. QUASH the rebellion.
    fear — stir up — laugh at — oppose — crush
15. SLOVENLY people.
    hateful — poor — careful — untidy — wonderful

BENEVOLENT (bə-nev′-ə-lənt) adj.: kindly, good, humane

The *bene* part of BENEVOLENT means *good* or *well;* it is also used in words like *benefit* and *benefactor*. The *vol* part of the word means *wish*. A BENEVOLENT person wishes other people well; he wants to make other people happy, and therefore is generous and kindly. See *-ant* under Suffixes.

"The BENEVOLENT woman worked as a volunteer in a hospital and gave thousands of dollars to charity."

BENEVOLENT is also used about people's actions and attitudes, and about places that exist to do good works.

"The teacher took a BENEVOLENT attitude toward her students, and tried to help them in every way she could."

"The BENEVOLENT institution provides toys for poor children at Christmastime."

Other forms of the word: BENEVOLENCE, n.

GUISE (gīz) n.: outward appearance, aspect, semblance

The GUISE of something is its outward appearance, the way it looks. The word may often suggest that this appearance is false or misleading.

"The prince walked through the city streets in the GUISE of a poor beggar."

"Under the GUISE of friendship he offered to help them find the money; he really wanted to keep it all for himself."

To DISGUISE something is to change its appearance or GUISE.

"The thief got into the house by DISGUISING himself as a mailman."

Other forms of the word: DISGUISE, n., v.

CONTRIVE (kən-trīv′) v.: to invent, design, concoct; to manage or devise a way

To CONTRIVE something or to CONTRIVE to do it is to find a way of doing it. The word suggests the use of cleverness in achieving something that may be rather difficult.

"She CONTRIVED a device that would open locked doors without a key."

"He CONTRIVED to get both the enemies into one room together to discuss their differences."

"The author CONTRIVED a happy ending for his novel."

The adjective CONTRIVED is used about things that show too clearly that they are planned and artificial.

"His remarks were clever but rather CONTRIVED, as if he had rehearsed them all beforehand."

Other forms of the word: CONTRIVANCE, n.
CONTRIVED, adj.

DEPICT (di-pikt′) v.: to describe, represent

DEPICT is related to the word *picture*. To DEPICT something is to draw it or describe it, to make a picture of it. Something can be DEPICTED in a real picture, in words, on stage, etc.

"The painting DEPICTS the king as a young man."

"He is DEPICTED in the novel as a mean, vicious scoundrel."

"The actress tried to DEPICT the emotions of the character she was playing."

"The writer DEPICTED the horrors of war."

Other forms of the word: DEPICTION, n.

JAUNDICED (jôn′-dist) adj.: yellowish; hostile, prejudiced, jealous

JAUNDICE is a disease which turns the skin yellow. JAUNDICED skin or a JAUNDICED appearance, therefore, looks as if it has been affected by JAUNDICE: it is yellow or yellowish.

JAUNDICE can affect the vision, and people with JAUNDICE sometimes see things as being yellow. JAUNDICED has therefore come to be used about people who see things as being worse than they are, because of envy, suspicion, prejudice, and so on.

"He looked with a somewhat JAUNDICED eye on their plan to hitchhike across the country"—that is, he wasn't very much in favor of it, and thought it would turn out badly.

Other forms of the word: JAUNDICE, n.

PENSIVE (pen′-siv) adj.: thoughtful, deep in thought

Someone who is PENSIVE is deep in thought. Often PENSIVE suggests a dreamy kind of thoughtfulness, where a person isn't reasoning a problem through but is simply in a reflective, almost sad mood.

"She sat there for a long time with a PENSIVE, faraway look on her face."

"Jim became rather PENSIVE whenever he remembered those sad incidents in his life."

SQUANDER (skwon′-dər) v.: to waste, spend carelessly, throw away foolishly

To SQUANDER something is to waste it, to use it up extravagantly and carelessly. The word is used especially about time and money. People who are careful about saving money do not SQUANDER it.

"He SQUANDERED his pay on gambling."

"When the day of the test came, she was sorry that she had SQUANDERED all of her time watching television."

"She SQUANDERED her life on foolish pleasures."

ULTERIOR (u̅hl-tEr′-E-ər) adj.: hidden, not obvious, unseen

ULTERIOR comes from a Latin word that means *lying beyond, lying further off.* In English the word usually has the sense "being beyond what is seen or admitted" and suggests that something is purposely being kept concealed. The word is generally used about purposes, motives, and the like.

"Not a shadow of his ULTERIOR purpose was visible in his actions."

"He pretended to be friendly toward the others, but I knew that he had an ULTERIOR motive for it."

"The child was so open and innocent that one could not suspect him of having ULTERIOR thoughts."

AMASS (ə-mas′) v.: to gather, accumulate, pile up

To AMASS is to pile up into a mass, to heap up or accumulate. The word is usually, although not always, used about something that is valuable.

"He AMASSED huge amounts of gold."

"I AMASSED a great deal of knowledge during high school."

"Jim AMASSED thousands of bottlecaps over the years."

"Jane AMASSED a fortune by buying and selling stocks."

KINDRED (kin′-drid) adj.: related, similar

Your KIN are your family, your relatives.

"Her KIN stood by her when everyone else had deserted her."

KINDRED, as a noun, is another word for KIN.

"All his KINDRED came to visit him when he was ill."

As an adjective, KINDRED means "having a common source," *related.*

"English and German are KINDRED languages."

KINDRED also means "having much in common," *similar.*

"They were KINDRED spirits; they had the same opinions about almost everything."

ORDINANCE (ôr′-də-nəns) n.: an order, law, rule

ORDINANCE is related to the word *order.* An ORDINANCE is a law or rule, usually one issued by a city or town.

"The city council passed an ORDINANCE forbidding smoking in public places."

"There is a local ORDINANCE that makes littering punishable by a fifty dollar fine."

KNOLL (nOl) n.: a small hill, mound

A KNOLL is a small hill, usually with a rounded shape.

"The land was flat except for a few gentle KNOLLS in the distance."

"It took us only a minute or two to climb to the top of the KNOLL."

ORIFICE (ôr′-ə-fis) n.: an opening, mouth, aperture

ORIFICE comes from the Latin word for *mouth,* also the source of the word *oral.* ORIFICE is used for any outer opening or mouth of something.

"The ORIFICE of the tube had become blocked up with dirt."

"The creature had a small ORIFICE through which it took in food and air."

QUASH (kwosh) v.: to put an end to, beat down, crush

QUASH is related to the word *squash,* and both have about the same meaning: to *beat down, crush.* QUASH, however, is used more about rebellions, chances, hopes, rumors, and the like, than about physical objects.

"The army QUASHED the rebellion easily."

"The airplane strike QUASHED our hopes of getting home for Christmas."

SLOVENLY (sluhv′-ən-lE) adj.: untidy, sloppy, careless

A SLOVEN is a person who always dresses, acts, or works in a messy, slipshod manner. SLOVENLY is the adjective from SLOVEN. (It is an adjective even though it ends in *-ly.*) A person is SLOVENLY if he is sloppy or careless about his appearance or work.

"She is so SLOVENLY. She looks as though she sleeps in her clothes."

"Jim's SLOVENLY appearance makes a very bad impression on people."

SLOVENLY is also used about people's activities and products.

"It was a SLOVENLY report, full of mistakes and erasures."

"The supervisor criticized the mechanic's SLOVENLY workmanship."

Other forms of the word: SLOVEN, n.

Exercise 1

Answer each question with a YES or NO. Put a check in the space for YES or NO next to the question.

	Yes	No
EXAMPLE Is a speck of dust TINY?	✓	
1. Would a BENEVOLENT person be stingy?		✓
2. Would an actor appear in different GUISES on stage?	✓	
3. Did Thomas Edison CONTRIVE things?	✓	
4. Can a person be DEPICTED in a short story?	✓	
5. Are cheerful people usually JAUNDICED?		✓
6. Would someone who is in a PENSIVE mood be very talkative?		✓
7. Do people become rich by SQUANDERING their money?		✓
8. Could people with ULTERIOR motives be called sneaky?	✓	
9. Can you AMASS facts?	✓	
10. Are apes and gorillas KINDRED animals?	✓	
11. Are you supposed to obey an ORDINANCE?	✓	
12. Is it difficult to reach the top of a KNOLL?		✓
13. Can an ORIFICE be very small?	✓	
14. If you QUASH a rumor, would you confirm that it is true?		✓
15. Would a SLOVENLY person make a good waiter?		✓

Exercise 2

Each sentence contains a test word in CAPITAL letters. Decide whether the test word is being used correctly or incorrectly in the sentence. Put a check in the space for RIGHT or WRONG next to the sentence.

	Right	Wrong
EXAMPLE After working hard all day Bill felt TINY and wanted to sleep.		✓
1. With a BENEVOLENT sneer he laughed at her misfortune.		✓
2. In the GUISE of a policeman the spy could go anywhere he wanted in the building.	✓	
3. She CONTRIVED to get her husband home in time for the surprise party.	✓	
4. She tried to DEPICT everyday life in ancient Russia for them.	✓	
5. He had a JAUNDICED view of government; he thought every politican was a crook.	✓	
6. Whenever she was in a PENSIVE mood she would think of all the exciting things she was missing in life.	✓	

		Right	Wrong
7.	Bill SQUANDERED his artistic talent on drawing cartoons for advertisements.	✓	
8.	They examined the ULTERIOR of the house for any signs of water damage.		✓
9.	She AMASSED a large collection of fine paintings.	✓	
10.	Everyone was so KINDRED to me that I forgot all about my problems.		✓
11.	The ORDINANCE in Bill's family was to have Thanksgiving dinner early in the afternoon.	✓	
12.	We picnicked at the foot of a small KNOLL.	✓	
13.	Mrs. Smith went to work at the ORIFICE every day.		✓
14.	The disabled airplane fell down and QUASHED the water.		✓
15.	We were shocked by his SLOVENLY appearance; he just didn't seem to care how he looked.	✓	

Exercise 3

Each test word is followed by three other words. Decide which of the three words is LEAST CLOSELY RELATED in its meaning to the meaning of the test word. Put the letter for the word you choose in the space at the end of the line.

EXAMPLE

	TINY:	a) small	b) short	c) angry	C
1.	BENEVOLENT:	a) beautiful	b) charitable	c) generous	A
2.	GUISE:	a) resemblance	b) interference	c) appearance	B
3.	CONTRIVE:	a) devise	b) defeat	c) design	B
4.	DEPICT:	a) represent	b) improve	c) paint	B
5.	JAUNDICED:	a) suspicious	b) yellow	c) uncertain	A
6.	PENSIVE:	a) active	b) reflective	c) meditative	A
7.	SQUANDER:	a) spend	b) forget	c) waste	B
8.	ULTERIOR:	a) secret	b) unknown	c) dangerous	C
9.	AMASS:	a) choose	b) accumulate	c) collect	A
10.	KINDRED:	a) similar	b) related	c) identical	C
11.	ORDINANCE:	a) law	b) suggestion	c) regulation	B
12.	KNOLL:	a) mound	b) plain	c) hill	B
13.	ORIFICE:	a) hole	b) corridor	c) mouth	B
14.	QUASH:	a) put down	b) wear out	c) destroy	B
15.	SLOVENLY:	a) dangerous	b) messy	c) slipshod	A

Chapter 6

Pretest

Each test word is printed in CAPITAL letters in a phrase. From the five choices on the next line, select the one which comes nearest in meaning to the meaning of the test word. Underline the one you select.

1.	The FACADE of the building.				
	basement	rear	front	structure	first floor
2.	It had been ADULTERATED.				
	substituted	made impure	made stronger	shaken up	aged
3.	CLEAVE it.				
	turn	smooth	bend	crack	split
4.	He ENUMERATED the problems.				
	knew about	found	listed	added to	talked about
5.	Finally AFFIXED.				
	fastened	repaired	removed	finished	improved
6.	See the PRECIPICE.				
	valley	cliff	pathway	roof	stairway
7.	Stood AGAPE.				
	laughing	wide open	horrified	at ease	firm
8.	They were SUBMISSIVE.				
	determined	friendly	tame	silent	wild
9.	Their ANTAGONISM.				
	fear	suffering	attraction	contest	hostility
10.	Obvious APPENDAGE.				
	rubbish	conclusion	class	attachment	treatment
11.	Where is his DOMICILE?				
	servant	office	home	birthplace	weapon
12.	Heard the GUFFAW.				
	noisy laugh	shout	short answer	bitter cry	sneeze
13.	Uncovered STRATA.				
	layers	walls	information	depths	scratches
14.	Watch the BUFFOON.				
	monkey	hurricane	juggler	clown	singer
15.	To ADVOCATE a plan.				
	discuss	recommend	abandon	accept	criticize

FACADE (fə-sahd') n.: the front (of a building); a false appearance

Note the pronunciation. The *c* is soft.

The FACADE of a building is its front, the part which faces the street and which most people see.

> "The bomb damaged the FACADE of the hotel, but the people inside were unharmed."

Sometimes, to make a small building appear to be bigger than it actually is, the FACADE is extended above the building's top floor. Such a FACADE is called a *false front.*

> "The FACADE of the building is two stories high, but the building has only one floor."

From this meaning FACADE has come to be used for any outward appearance, especially one which is false or misleading.

> "She looked calm, but this was just a FACADE; she was really very angry."
>
> "Their apparent wealth was all a FACADE; in fact, they could barely afford the clothes they wore."

Usage: FACADE is also sometimes spelled *façade.*

CLEAVE (klEv) v.: to split, tear, cut apart

To CLEAVE something is to split it apart, especially with a cutting blow—for example, from an ax.

> "He could CLEAVE the log with one mighty swing of his ax."
>
> "The force of the explosion CLEAVED the boulder in two."

CLEAVE can also be used about the thing being cut.

> "This kind of wood CLEAVES easily."

In a slightly different sense, the word can also mean "to make way for, by (or as if by) cutting."

> "They CLEAVED a path through the jungle."

A CLEAVER is a heavy instrument used by butchers to cut up animals.

Other forms of the word: CLEAVER, n.

Usage: CLEAVE is a rather formal word, used more in print than in speech. The past tense of CLEAVE can be CLEAVED, CLOVE, or CLEFT. Interestingly, CLEAVE has a second meaning that is almost the opposite of the meaning given above; it means "to cling to or be firmly attached to," as in "The wet uniforms cleaved to their bodies."

ADULTERATE (ə-duhl'-tər-At) v.: to make impure, corrupt, pollute

ADULTERATE has nothing to do with the word *adult.* To ADULTERATE something is to make it less pure, usually by adding a substance that is of poorer quality. The word is used especially about foods and drugs.

> "He claimed the hamburger had been ADULTERATED by the addition of harmful chemicals."

The word is also sometimes used in a general sense.

> "Her happiness was ADULTERATED by the continuing suspicion that it was all about to end."

The word UNADULTERATED means *pure* or *sheer.*

> "Everything he says is UNADULTERATED nonsense"—that is, it is complete and total nonsense.

Other forms of the word: ADULTERATION, n.
UNADULTERATED, adj.

ENUMERATE (i-nU'-mər-At) v.: to count, list, name one by one

ENUMERATE comes from the same Latin source as *number, numeral, numerous,* and other words having to do with numbers and counting. ENUMERATE can mean simply to *count,* but it usually has the sense of "counting off" or listing items one after another.

> "He began to ENUMERATE the reasons why we shouldn't go."
>
> "We ENUMERATED the qualities we thought the new employee should have."

In most cases it is better to use the simpler words *count* and *list,* unless the sense is specifically to count off one after another.

Other forms of the word: ENUMERATION, n.

AFFIX (ə-fiks') v.: to attach, fasten, stick firmly in place

To AFFIX something is to attach it to something else.

"You must AFFIX a stamp to that letter or else the post office won't deliver it."

The AFFIXING doesn't have to be a physical act.

"The teacher AFFIXED a severe penalty to cheating on the test."

"He AFFIXED great importance to the professor's remarks."

AFFIX is often used about adding your signature to something.

"He had to AFFIX his signature to the bottom of the document to make it legal."

AFFIX comes from the same source as the word *fix*. AFFIX has nothing to do with *fix* in the sense of *repair*. *Fix*, though, can mean "to put firmly in place" as in the phrase "to *fix* in your memory." The two words in this sense have close to the same meaning.

PRECIPICE (pres'-ə-pis) n.: a steep cliff

A PRECIPICE is a very steep cliff, one that has almost a vertical face to it.

"Everyone was afraid to go very near the edge of the PRECIPICE."

"The mountain climbers decided it would be almost impossible to reach the top of the PRECIPICE."

Sometimes PRECIPICE is used in a general sense for the brink of any kind of disaster.

"The nation now stands on the PRECIPICE of a severe economic depression."

In the Pretest, many people choose *valley* as the meaning of PRECIPICE. A PRECIPICE is a cliff which might lead down into a *valley*, but it is not the *valley* itself.

AGAPE (ə-gAp') adj.: wide open, gaping; in a state of wonder.

AGAPE is related to the words *gap* and *gape*. The word means *wide open*. It is usually used about a person's mouth, which might be open because of wonder, surprise, a yawn, or the like.

"His mouth was AGAPE when he saw who had walked in the door."

"The crowd was AGAPE at the astounding feats of the acrobats."

Many people choose *horrified* as the synonym for AGAPE. A person's mouth may be AGAPE because of horror, but the word means *wide open*, not *horrified*.

Usage: AGAPE always comes after the noun it modifies.

SUBMISSIVE (suhb-mis'-iv) adj.: tame, yielding, compliant, docile

SUBMISSIVE is an adjective from SUBMIT. See *-ive* under Suffixes. One meaning of SUBMIT is "to yield to someone else's authority, to surrender."

"When the police arrived, the burglar submitted without a struggle."

Someone who is SUBMISSIVE is inclined to SUBMIT, to yield to power or authority.

"They were very SUBMISSIVE children. They would obey anyone who gave them an order."

"Why are you so SUBMISSIVE? You shouldn't do everything he tells you to do."

Other forms of the word: SUBMIT, v.
SUBMISSION, n.

ANTAGONISM (an-tag'-ə-nizm) n.: hostility, opposition, enmity

ANTAGONISM is active opposition, between people or groups, for example, who are unfriendly or in conflict. The word usually suggests a basic dislike which can easily be stirred up into actual fighting.

"The natives felt an ANTAGONISM toward the tourists who swarmed into their town every summer."

"Jim's mother tried to end the ANTAGONISM between his brother and him."

Many people pick *suffering* as the meaning of ANTAGONISM, probably because they see the word *agony* in ANTAGONISM. Actually, both words come from a Greek word meaning *struggle*, but they have developed very different meanings.

Other forms of the word: ANTAGONIST, n.
ANTAGONISTIC, adj.
ANTAGONIZE, v.

APPENDAGE (ə-pen′-dij) n.: an attachment, accessory, addition

The *pend* part of APPENDAGE comes from the Latin word for *hang,* also the source of English words like *pendant* and *pendulum.* An APPENDAGE is something that is attached or added on to something else so that it is part of it. See *ad-* under Prefixes. In biology, arms, legs, tails, and fins are appendages. In general use, however, the word usually suggests that this added-on part is not very important or essential.

"The shed was merely a small APPENDAGE of the large house."

"The fancy knobs and dials on the machine were useless APPENDAGES; they were just there to make it look impressive."

To APPEND something is to add or attach it to something else.

"A bibliography was APPENDED to the book before they published the second edition."

DOMICILE (dom′-ə-sIl or dOm′-ə-sIl) n.: a home, dwelling place, residence

A DOMICILE is a home or dwelling place. The word is especially used to mean "a person's legal residence"—that is, where he can be considered to live for voting or tax purposes.

"The judge ruled that her legal DOMICILE was in New York State."

"He decided to establish his DOMICILE in Cleveland"—in other words, he decided to live there.

DOMICILE is also a verb. To DOMICILE is to reside or dwell.

"They DOMICILED in the south of the country during the winter months."

GUFFAW (gə-fô′) n.: a noisy burst of laughter

A GUFFAW is a loud, coarse laugh. Originally the word was probably just an imitation of the sound of this kind of laugh.

"The comedian's act certainly didn't produce any GUFFAWS in the audience; all we could hear were a few scattered giggles."

GUFFAW can also be used as a verb.

"The audience GUFFAWED when the villain slipped on a banana peel."

The most commonly chosen wrong answer on the Pretest is *bitter cry,* which is opposite in meaning to GUFFAW.

STRATA (strA′-tə or stra′-tə) n.: layers, levels

STRATA is the plural of STRATUM. A STRATUM is an even layer of something. STRATA are several of these layers, one on top of the other. The word is most often used about layers of rocks, but it is also used about other things like social classes.

"Geologists can study the history of the Earth by examining the STRATA of rock formations."

"Various STRATA of society were represented on the committee."

BUFFOON (bə-fUn′) n.: a clown, jester

A BUFFOON is a *clown,* someone who says or does foolish things to entertain people.

"The BUFFOON stood on his head and barked like a dog to amuse the king."

In general, BUFFOON is an insulting term for any extremely stupid or foolish person.

"He called his opponent a BUFFOON and said he was too stupid to be president."

BUFFOONERY is clown-like behavior.

"Stop all this BUFFOONERY and act your age."

The most commonly chosen wrong answer is *monkey,* probably because of confusion with *baboon,* which is a kind of *monkey.*

Other forms of the word: BUFFOONERY, n.

ADVOCATE (ad′-və-kAt) v.: to recommend, support

To ADVOCATE something is to speak or write publicly in favor of it.

"She ADVOCATES a shorter school day and longer vacations for students."

"Everyone at the meeting seemed to ADVOCATE a different way of solving the problem."

"No one on the committee ADVOCATED doing away with taxes entirely."

ADVOCATE is also a noun. An ADVOCATE is someone who defends or pleads for a cause or a person.

"The plan's strongest ADVOCATES are the ones who will gain the most from it."

Other forms of the word: ADVOCACY, n.

Exercise 1

Answer each question with a YES or NO. Put a check in the space for YES or NO next to the question.

		Yes	No
EXAMPLE	Is a speck of dust TINY?	✓	
1.	Is the FACADE of a building on the outside?		
2.	Is food better after it has been ADULTERATED?		
3.	Can an ax CLEAVE a piece of wood?		
4.	If you ENUMERATE the difficulties of a plan, do you cause more of them?		
5.	Could glue be used to AFFIX a poster to a wall?		
6.	Is it dangerous to be on the edge of a PRECIPICE?		
7.	Would a person's mouth be AGAPE while he is yawning?		
8.	Would a SUBMISSIVE person be easy to get along with?		
9.	Do close friends feel a strong ANTAGONISM toward each other?		
10.	Are APPENDAGES usually very necessary?		
11.	If you permanently moved to another state, could you keep the same DOMICILE?		
12.	Would people GUFFAW at a funeral?		
13.	Do STRATA lie beside one another?		
14.	Are BUFFOONS supposed to be funny?		
15.	Would a salesman ADVOCATE buying his product?		

Exercise 2

Each sentence contains a test word in CAPITAL letters. Decide whether the test word is being used correctly or incorrectly in the sentence. Put a check in the space for RIGHT or WRONG next to the sentence.

		Right	Wrong
EXAMPLE	After working hard all day Bill felt TINY and wanted to sleep.		✓
1.	His FACADE of indifference disguised his concern.		
2.	That television show is UNADULTERATED trash; it's the worst program I've ever seen.		
3.	She CLEAVED the windows with a bucket of water and a sponge.		
4.	She quickly ENUMERATED the advantages her idea had over all the rest.		
5.	John would have to AFFIX the car whenever it broke down.		
6.	The plane was forced to land in a deep PRECIPICE.		
7.	The boys stood AGAPE when they saw the ghost suddenly appear.		

	Right	Wrong
8. Some teachers are too SUBMISSIVE; they won't let you get away with anything.		✓
9. He lay on the ground in ANTAGONISM after he had been wounded.		✓
10. Jim wanted to be an important part of the team, but the coach made him feel as if he were just an APPENDAGE.	✓	
11. He worked in Los Angeles, but his DOMICILE was outside the city.	✓	
12. His joke brought a loud GUFFAW from everyone.	✓	
13. The highest STRATUM of their society sets the fashion for the other classes.	✓	
14. He called us a bunch of BUFFOONS for acting so silly during the class.	✓	
15. The senator was a strong ADVOCATE of the Equal Rights Amendment.	✓	

Exercise 3

Each test word is followed by three other words. Decide which of the three words is LEAST CLOSELY RELATED in its meaning to the meaning of the test word. Put the letter for the word you choose in the space at the end of the line.

EXAMPLE

TINY:	a) small	b) short	c) angry	C
1. FACADE:	a) show	b) appearance	c) shine	C
2. ADULTERATE:	a) worsen	b) corrupt	c) remove	C
3. CLEAVE:	a) separate	b) rip	c) ruin	C
4. ENUMERATE:	a) count	b) list	c) increase	C
5. AFFIX:	a) pile	b) connect	c) stick	A
6. PRECIPICE :	a) side	b) cliff	c) brink	A
7. AGAPE:	a) ajar	b) open	c) huge	C
8. SUBMISSIVE:	a) yielding	b) tame	c) thoughtful	C
9. ANTAGONISM:	a) fear	b) opposition	c) conflict	A
10. APPENDAGE:	a) improvement	b) addition	c) attachment	A
11. DOMICILE:	a) home	b) shop	c) house	B
12. GUFFAW:	a) smile	b) chuckle	c) laugh	A
13. STRATA:	a) angles	b) rows	c) levels	A
14. BUFFOON:	a) fool	b) thief	c) comedian	B
15. ADVOCATE:	a) tolerate	b) defend	c) favor	A

Review Test 2—Chapters 4–6

Fill in each blank with the test word (or a form of the test word) which best fits the sentence. Use the words listed below.

AGAPE	DOMICILE	MELEE	PLACATE	STRATA
ALOOF	GUFFAW	ORIFICE	QUIRK	SUBMISSIVE
BENEVOLENT	KINDRED	PANG	SQUANDER	SWOON
BLASPHEME	MANIFOLD	PENSIVE	STEADFAST	VEHEMENT
CONTRIVE				

1. Their theories of education are ______________; they have much in common, although they're not exactly alike.
2. As they dug deeper they uncovered several ______________ of ruins, indicating that the city had been rebuilt many times.
3. Although everyone was certain that he had been killed, she remained ______________ in her belief that someday he would return.
4. Mr. Jones ______________ his life's savings on a scheme he thought would make him wealthy.
5. Mary almost ______________ when the handsome movie star kissed her.
6. With a(n) ______________ shake of her head, Jane denied that she had stolen the money.
7. At first the boy seemed rebellious, but he was really very ______________ and would do whatever he was told.
8. He cleverly ______________ to get paid for work he would have had to do for free anyway.
9. Jim tried to ______________ his father by washing the car, but his father stayed angry.
10. In her despair she ______________ God and called Him evil.
11. His stories were so funny that all you could hear were loud ______________ in the room.
12. He felt a(n) ______________ of envy when he saw his opponent receive the award.
13. Ed has an annoying ______________ of pretending to be in deep thought whenever you ask him the simplest question.
14. Our mouths were ______________ when we heard that we had won the contest.
15. He spent much of his time outside the country, but his legal ______________ was New York City.
16. Late at night he would become rather ______________ and start thinking about the meaning of life.
17. Even though everyone tried to get him to be friendly, he remained ______________ and said he was too busy for friendship.
18. The microbe took in air through a small ______________ in its side.
19. The town meeting became a confused ______________ as one person after another stood up and demanded to be heard.
20. The ______________ man helped thousands of needy people.
21. There was a list three pages long of the ______________ duties Sharon had in her important new job.

Fill in each blank with the test word (or a form of the test word) which best fits the sentence. Use the words listed below.

ADULTERATE	ANTAGONISM	ENUMERATE	JAUNDICED	PROCURE
ADVOCATE	APPENDAGE	FACADE	KNOLL	QUASH
AFFIX	BUFFOON	GUISE	NONPAREIL	SLOVENLY
ALLOT	CLEAVE	HALLOWED	ORDINANCE	ULTERIOR
AMASS	DEPICT	IMPLORE	PRECIPICE	

22. All of us hold sacred the __________ memory of our dead mother.
23. He told us that the car was so old it was impossible to __________ the parts to repair it.
24. With his sharp ax he managed to __________ the log with one stroke.
25. The nature committee __________ turning the area into a state park.
26. They acted like __________, singing silly songs and playing foolish pranks.
27. The company __________ the maple syrup by adding some cheaper liquids to it.
28. The sick man appeared __________. The doctor suggested that fresh air and sunlight would improve his color.
29. They maintain a(n) __________ of happiness, but really they are both very miserable.
30. It is impossible at this time to __________ all the reasons why we are doing this.
31. He was so __________ that he wouldn't wash the dishes or take out the rubbish. His entire house was a mess.
32. The police were called in to __________ the riot, and they put an end to it almost as soon as it started.
33. We were each __________ a portion of the garden in which to grow vegetables.
34. Jane got dizzy when she stood at the edge of the __________ and looked down at the ground far below.
35. The movie __________ him as a handsome, brave fellow, but he wasn't like that at all.
36. This is merely a(n) __________ of the larger work, added on to it much later.
37. Can't we do something to reduce the __________ between those two students? They always look as if they're ready to kill each other.
38. The lawyer __________ a considerable amount of evidence to use at the trial.
39. Wendy __________ a star to the top of the Christmas tree.
40. He __________ the robber not to take his watch, but the robber ignored his pleas.
41. Her cooking is __________; I've never tasted food that good before.
42. Under the __________ of a political survey the study actually probed people's religious beliefs.
43. She must have had some __________ purpose in visiting us. She wouldn't come all this way just to say hello.
44. Jim lay at the top of a small grassy __________ and stared at the sky.
45. The city issued a new __________ that made it illegal to park on the street overnight.

Chapter 7

Pretest

Each test word is printed in CAPITAL letters in a phrase. From the five choices on the next line, select the one which comes nearest in meaning to the meaning of the test word. Underline the one you select.

1. A real DESPOT.
   dungeon | tyrant | saint | fat man | station
2. GENTEEL behavior.
   strict | amusing | calm | polite | rude
3. Very INSUBORDINATE.
   unfriendly | stingy | disobedient | well behaved | outstanding
4. Impressive GIRTH.
   wit | depth | speed | value | size
5. Sudden INTERJECTION.
   conversation | excitement | idea | exclamation | removal
6. To REBUKE him.
   cheat | hurt | praise | scold | ignore
7. LISTLESS person.
   lost | ignorant | spiritless | penniless | fearless
8. Much PARAPHERNALIA.
   rejoicing | equipment | poverty | clothing | confusion
9. Certain REPERCUSSIONS.
   effects | noises | injuries | differences | reasons
10. VIABLE projects.
    impossible | workable | wonderful | unusual | changeable
11. Full of BAUBLES.
    beads | gifts | diamonds | rings | trinkets
12. Difficult to ATTAIN.
    hold | stop | see | know | reach
13. He BERATED the employee.
    scolded | discharged | praised | evaluated | struck
14. Ignored the CONSENSUS.
    idea | debate | listing | agreement | election
15. They remained IMPASSIVE.
    uncertain | excited | unmoved | tired | active

DESPOT (des′-pət or des′-pot) n.: a tyrant, absolute ruler

DESPOT was originally an honorary title applied to the emperor of Byzantium. From this the word came to be used about any ruler with absolute and unlimited powers. Nowadays DESPOT usually suggests a ruler who uses these powers unjustly or cruelly.

"The DESPOT imprisoned everyone who criticized him."

"The owner of the company used to be fairly reasonable, but lately he has become a real DESPOT, demanding complete obedience in everything."

The actions or character of a DESPOT are called DESPOTIC.

"The king's DESPOTIC treatment of the peasants caused them to revolt."

Other forms of the word: DESPOTIC, adj.
DESPOTISM, n.

GENTEEL (jen-tEl′) adj.: polite, well bred, refined

GENTEEL is related to the word *gentle*, but the words have taken on very different meanings and should not be confused. GENTEEL means "having the style or characteristics of the upper class," *refined, well bred.*

"The two very GENTEEL ladies were shocked by the filthiness of the house."

GENTEEL is usually used with a slightly sarcastic sense, as if the politeness and good breeding were put on or out of place. The word is often found in the phrase "GENTEEL poverty," which refers to people who try to maintain the style of the upper classes, even though they are too poor to do this very well.

INSUBORDINATE (in-sə-bôr′-də-nit) adj.: disobedient, rebellious

See *in-*$_2$ and *sub-* under Prefixes and *ate*$_2$ under Suffixes. A person who is a SUBORDINATE is in a lower position than someone else, and he has to obey the people who are above him.

"He is a poor boss. He treats his SUBORDINATES as if they didn't have any feelings."

Someone who is INSUBORDINATE is unwilling to be a SUBORDINATE. He is disobedient and rebels against authority.

"Some of my employees were so INSUBORDINATE that I had to fire them."

"The private was accused of being INSUBORDINATE to an officer."

Other forms of the word: INSUBORDINATION, n.

GIRTH (gerth) n. circumference, size

GIRTH comes from an old word for *belt.* A GIRTH is the belt that goes around a horse to keep the saddle in place. GIRTH has come to mean the measurement *around* something, especially the measurement around a person's body.

"For a short person he has a very large GIRTH; it is difficult to find a pair of pants that fit him."

"They tried to estimate the GIRTH of the tree trunk before they actually measured it."

"His huge GIRTH made it difficult for him to get in and out of cars."

INTERJECTION (in-tər-jek′-shən) n.: an exclamation

See *inter-* under Prefixes. The *ject* part of the word means *throw.* It is also found in words like *project* and *reject.* To INTERJECT means to *throw in* a comment or remark in the middle of what someone else is saying.

" 'But that's not true!' he INTERJECTED in the middle of the professor's speech."

An INTERJECTION is a word or phrase suddenly shouted out in excitement. *Wow! Stop! Oh, no! Go ahead!* are all examples of INTERJECTIONS.

Other forms of the word: INTERJECT, v.

REBUKE (ri-byUk′) v.: to scold, criticize, censure

To REBUKE someone is to criticize him sharply, to speak severely to him.

"The teacher REBUKED him for speaking out of turn."

"She was REBUKED by her parents for staying out late."

REBUKE is also a noun, meaning "a strong expression of disapproval," a *reproof.*

"She received a strong REBUKE for not making her bed."

LISTLESS (list′-ləs) adj.: spiritless, indifferent

See *-less* under Suffixes. The *list* part of the word comes from an old word meaning *desire.* Someone who is LISTLESS lacks desire; he is too bored or tired to do anything. The word is used about people's moods, appearance, and actions.

"The girl has been in a LISTLESS mood all day. She won't do anything; she just lies on her bed and stares at the ceiling."

"He greeted them with a LISTLESS handshake which showed he wasn't very interested in meeting them."

"Pete made a LISTLESS attempt to do his homework, then gave up and went back to watching television."

PARAPHERNALIA (par-ə-fər-nAl-yə) n.: equipment, apparatus, furnishings

PARAPHERNALIA is the equipment used for a particular kind of job or a particular purpose.

"A baseball player's PARAPHERNALIA includes bat, ball, glove, and uniform."

"The fishermen stowed all their PARAPHERNALIA under the seats of the boat."

"When he first entered the laboratory, he didn't know what half of the PARAPHERNALIA was."

REPERCUSSION (rE-pər-kush′-ən or re-pər-kush′-ən) n.: an effect, result, consequence

See *re-* under Prefixes. The *percuss* part of the word comes from a Latin word meaning to *strike. Percussion* instruments are musical instruments, like drums and cymbals, which make sounds by being struck. A REPERCUSSION is a striking or beating back, such as when a body hits another body that resists it. The word is usually used in a general sense about the effects, often indirect or widespread, of a particular action.

"There will certainly be REPERCUSSIONS if we decide to fire him."

"No one knew what the REPERCUSSIONS of this decision would be."

"The REPERCUSSIONS of his speech were felt far and wide."

VIABLE (vI′-ə-bəl) adj.: capable of living; workable

See *-able* under Suffixes. The *vi* part of VIABLE comes from the French word *vie,* which means *life.* Something which is VIABLE is able to live or exist, is capable of surviving. The word is used about unborn babies who have developed enough to be capable of living outside the womb. In a sense that has developed from this, VIABLE means "capable of being done," *workable.*

"His plan was clever but not particularly VIABLE. It would cost a lot and require a great deal of work."

"After some initial problems, their agreement proved to be quite VIABLE."

Changeable is the most commonly chosen wrong answer in the Pretest, probably because VIABLE is confused with the word *variable.*

BAUBLE (bô′-bəl) n.: a trinket, plaything, ornament

A BAUBLE is a bright, pretty object that has little or no usefulness. It may or may not be expensive.

"He bought some little BAUBLE for the child to keep her occupied during the long trip."

"She bought several shiny BAUBLES just because she liked the look of them."

"He said the jewel was just a BAUBLE that he hoped she liked."

ATTAIN (ə-tAn′) v.: to reach, achieve, gain

To ATTAIN something is to gain it or reach it. The word generally suggests that some effort was needed, or that what was gained was valuable.

"You must study if you wish to ATTAIN knowledge."

"She ATTAINED her present high position by hard work and talent."

"It will be impossible to ATTAIN our goal without more help."

Hold is the most common mistake as the meaning of ATTAIN. This is probably due to confusion between ATTAIN and *retain.* To *retain* something is to hold on to it.

"Once he had ATTAINED power he did his best to *retain* it."

Other forms of the word: ATTAINMENT, n.

BERATE (bi-rAt') v.: to scold, rebuke, criticize sharply

To BERATE someone is to scold him sharply and angrily, often for an extended period of time.

"The teacher BERATED Tim for constantly being late."

"There is no need to BERATE the child. She already said she was sorry for her mistake."

"My mother is constantly BERATING me because my room is so messy."

CONSENSUS (kən-sen'-səs) n.: a general agreement, collective opinion

See *con-* under Prefixes. The *sens* part of the word means to *feel* or *think.* It comes from the same Latin word as *sense* and *sentiment.* A CONSENSUS is a *feeling together,* a general opinion shared by a number of people.

"It was the CONSENSUS of the group that much more work would have to be done."

"The class was unable to reach a CONSENSUS about the best place to have the Christmas party."

"The CONSENSUS of the coaches was that he was the best player in the league."

IMPASSIVE (im-pas'-əv) adj.: emotionless, unmoved, indifferent

Someone who is IMPASSIVE shows no signs of feeling or interest. He has no emotions, at least none that anyone can see.

"She remained IMPASSIVE while they told her of her mother's accident."

"He stared IMPASSIVELY at them as they threatened to torture him."

"Ken came back to the room with an IMPASSIVE look on his face. No one could tell whether he had passed or failed the test."

Exercise 1

Answer each question with a YES or NO. Put a check in the space for YES or NO next to the question.

	Yes	No
EXAMPLE Is a speck of dust TINY?	✓	
1. Are most DESPOTS kind?		
2. Would a savage be GENTEEL?		
3. Do teachers prefer INSUBORDINATE students?		
4. Is a person with a large GIRTH likely to weigh a lot?		
5. Is *Ouch!* an INTERJECTION?		
6. Would a teacher REBUKE a student for doing well on a test?		
7. Would LISTLESS people be a lot of fun at a party?		
8. Do mechanics have PARAPHERNALIA?		
9. Would a law to ban cars have REPERCUSSIONS in this country?		
10. Are VIABLE plans likely to fail?		
11. Is an automobile a BAUBLE?		
12. Do people want to ATTAIN their desires?		
13. Would a student be BERATED for getting an *A* in English?		
14. Does a unanimous vote represent a CONSENSUS?		
15. Are football fans usually IMPASSIVE?		

Exercise 2

Each sentence contains a test word in CAPITAL letters. Decide whether the test word is being used correctly or incorrectly in the sentence. Put a check in the space for RIGHT or WRONG next to the sentence.

	Right	Wrong
EXAMPLE After working hard all day Bill felt TINY and wanted to sleep.		✓
1. The country's DESPOTIC ruler had all his prisoners tortured.		
2. It's difficult to act in a GENTEEL manner when you are covered with mud.		
3. The boss claimed Art was being INSUBORDINATE, but Art said he had a right to express his opinions.		
4. By dieting she was able to decrease her GIRTH by six inches.		
5. She completely INTERJECTED any ideas that didn't agree with her own.		
6. The dog received a strong REBUKE whenever it barked in the house.		
7. Ed became LISTLESS and eager to get going whenever people were late.		

		Right	Wrong
8.	He had most of the usual PARAPHERNALIA for cleaning the house, but he couldn't find the vacuum cleaner.	___	___
9.	They had a long REPERCUSSION about the best way to raise money.	___	___
10.	Despite predictions of disaster, the new nation proved to be quite VIABLE, and actually flourished.	___	___
11.	He bought her a ring, bracelet, and some other BAUBLES for her birthday.	___	___
12.	He ATTAINED this house for five years before selling it.	___	___
13.	Frank's mother BERATED him for lying to her.	___	___
14.	Most people thought it was a great movie, but Jane's CONSENSUS was that it was terrible.	___	___
15.	They tried to make him laugh, but he continued to gaze IMPASSIVELY at them.	___	___

Exercise 3

Each test word is followed by three other words. Decide which of the three words is LEAST CLOSELY RELATED in its meaning to the meaning of the test word. Put the letter for the word you choose in the space at the end of the line.

EXAMPLE

	TINY:	a) small	b) short	c) angry	C
1.	DESPOT:	a) citizen	b) tyrant	c) ruler	___
2.	GENTEEL:	a) generous	b) noble	c) refined	___
3.	INSUBORDINATE:	a) rebellious	b) stupid	c) mutinous	___
4.	GIRTH:	a) width	b) size	c) height	___
5.	INTERJECTION:	a) exclamation	b) guess	c) shout	___
6.	REBUKE:	a) punish	b) debate	c) warn	___
7.	LISTLESS:	a) dull	b) bored	c) shy	___
8.	PARAPHERNALIA:	a) tools	b) houses	c) instruments	___
9.	REPERCUSSION:	a) result	b) importance	c) consequence	___
10.	VIABLE:	a) living	b) necessary	c) practical	___
11.	BAUBLE:	a) watch	b) trinket	c) toy	___
12.	ATTAIN:	a) obtain	b) win	c) keep	___
13.	BERATE:	a) denounce	b) criticize	c) mock	___
14.	CONSENSUS:	a) smell	b) opinion	c) agreement	___
15.	IMPASSIVE:	a) indifferent	b) emotionless	c) doubtful	___

Chapter 8

Pretest

Each test word is printed in CAPITAL letters in a phrase. From the five choices on the next line, select the one which comes nearest in meaning to the meaning of the test word. Underline the one you select.

1.	SAGE advice.				
	careful	wise	ancient	foolish	odd
2.	INDULGE the children.				
	accept	love	feed	pamper	punish
3.	To RECTIFY it.				
	change	enlarge	favor	correct	destroy
4.	Started the INSURRECTION.				
	fight	argument	uprising	trial	investigation
5.	REPREHENSIBLE behavior.				
	greedy	holy	puzzling	blameworthy	fearful
6.	A little SOLACE.				
	joy	strength	comfort	hope	sorrow
7.	Read his MEMOIRS.				
	life story	orders	short reminders	long novel	responses
8.	His RECOMPENSE.				
	mistake	duty	reputation	value	reward
9.	A certain TINGE.				
	sadness	trace	part	smell	change
10.	To VANQUISH them.				
	rescue	lose	defeat	hate	torture
11.	Its BREVITY.				
	length	decrease	value	weight	shortness
12.	Stopped the VENDETTA.				
	blood feud	sailing race	melody	police raid	truce
13.	DELETE the paragraph.				
	rearrange	shorten	finish	erase	include
14.	A great deal of MIRTH.				
	energy	light	excitement	sadness	merriment
15.	Disliked the RABBLE.				
	workers	enemy	nobility	mob	young

SAGE (sAj) adj.: wise, judicious

SAGE means *wise.* The word is especially applied to a person who is wise through long experience.

"The old judge was noted for his SAGE opinions."

"The SAGE teacher gave him good advice about how to solve the problem."

SAGE is also a noun, meaning "a profoundly wise man."

"The ancient SAGES knew a great deal about human nature."

INDULGE (in-duhlj') v.: to humor, pamper, spoil, give way to, gratify

To INDULGE someone is to satisfy his wishes and demands, even if he has little right to make them.

"Grandmother INDULGES those children too much. She lets them do whatever they want."

To INDULGE yourself is to give in to your own desires or feelings.

"After the long journey she INDULGED herself by taking a hot bath and eating at the best restaurant in town."

To INDULGE *in* something is to give in to your desire for it.

"They INDULGED in ice cream and cake after dinner."

"He INDULGES in the luxury of a cruise every year."

Other forms of the word: INDULGENCE, n.
INDULGENT, adj.

RECTIFY (rek'-tə-fI) v.: to correct, make right

The *rect* part of both RECTIFY and *correct* comes from a Latin word meaning *right.* Both words mean "to make or put right." See *-fy* under Suffixes.

"He tried to RECTIFY his mistake but only made it worse."

"She demanded that they RECTIFY their bad habits."

"If we cannot RECTIFY this problem soon we will have to end the entire project."

The most commonly chosen wrong answer in the Pretest is *change.* You can *change* something and make it wrong; to RECTIFY is only to make something right.

INSURRECTION (in-sə-rek'-shən) n.: an uprising, rebellion, revolt

INSURRECTION comes from a Latin word which means to *rise up* and which is also the source of the words *surge* and *insurgent.* An INSURRECTION is a rising up of people in resistance to authority or the government. It is usually less well organized than a rebellion or a revolution.

"The leaders of the INSURRECTION claimed that half the population supported their cause."

"The army crushed the INSURRECTION with little difficulty."

REPREHENSIBLE (re-pri-hen'-sə-bəl) adj.: blameworthy, deserving censure

See *-able* under Suffixes. REPREHEND is a rather uncommon word that means to *criticize,* to *reprove.* Someone or something that is REPREHENSIBLE deserves to be criticized.

"I think your actions were REPREHENSIBLE. You ought to be severely punished."

"His opinions are fine, but the way he forces everyone to agree with them is REPREHENSIBLE."

"Everyone thought the company's decision to make the work day longer was REPREHENSIBLE."

Puzzling is the most commonly chosen wrong answer on the Pretest, perhaps because REPREHENSIBLE looks like *incomprehensible,* which means *not understandable.*

SOLACE (sol'-əs) n.: comfort, consolation, relief

SOLACE means *comfort* or *relief* from sorrow or pain.

"He looked for SOLACE from his troubles."

SOLACE is also the thing that brings comfort.

"Her children were a SOLACE to her in her old age."

"The money her husband left her in his will was little SOLACE to her after his death."

"Nothing seemed to comfort him until he found some SOLACE in music."

MEMOIRS (mem′-wahrz) n.: a life story, autobiography, recollections

Note the pronunciation. MEMOIRS is a French word, and keeps the French pronunciation.

The word MEMOIRS is related to the word *memory*. MEMOIRS are a person's life story, usually telling about events and people that he has personal knowledge of.

"The general wrote his MEMOIRS about his experiences during the war."

"Everyone wanted to know what the movie star would say about these people in his MEMOIRS."

MEMOIRS is sometimes used in the singular.

"She wrote a MEMOIR of her early days in the fashion industry."

Short reminders is the most popular wrong answer on the Pretest, due to confusion with the word *memo*.

RECOMPENSE (rek′-əm-pens) n.: a reward, payment, compensation

A RECOMPENSE is a return or payment made for work, loss, or injury. The word suggests making up for something, an attempt to do justice or to make amends.

"He thought the RECOMPENSE they offered was not adequate for the loss of his home."

"The company gave her a Christmas bonus as partial RECOMPENSE for all the extra work she had done that year."

"We must make some RECOMPENSE for causing him to miss his plane flight."

RECOMPENSE is also a verb.

"The insurance company RECOMPENSED him for the theft of the camera."

TINGE (tinj) n.: a trace, slight coloring, slight mixture

TINGE may be used either as a noun or as a verb. A TINGE is a *trace* or *slight mixture* of something. The word is especially used about a slight trace of a color found in something, but it can also be used about traces of emotions in the face or voice.

"There is a TINGE of green in the sky."

"There was a TINGE of sadness in his expression as he walked out the door."

When used as a verb, TINGE means to *color* or *affect slightly*.

"The white tile floor was TINGED with yellow after only a few months."

"Her voice was TINGED with regret as she declined the invitation."

"The air was TINGED with the pleasant aroma of freshly baked bread."

VANQUISH (vang′-kwish) v.: to defeat, overcome, conquer.

VANQUISH means to *defeat* or *conquer*, but it is stronger than these words. VANQUISH usually suggests an important, complete defeat or conquest of an enemy.

"The victorious general had VANQUISHED the enemy."

One can VANQUISH other things besides enemies.

"The disease was totally VANQUISHED after they developed the new medicine."

"He was able to VANQUISH his fears about flying and board the plane."

BREVITY (brev′-ə-tE) n.: shortness, briefness

BREVITY is shortness of time. BREVITY is the noun usually used in association with the adjective *brief*.

"The program was very brief; we were surprised by its BREVITY."

"The poet mourned the BREVITY of human life."

"The BREVITY of this book was more than made up for by its wisdom and humor."

Many people choose *value* as the meaning of BREVITY, perhaps because BREVITY is usually considered to be a virtue.

VENDETTA (ven-det′-ə) n.: a blood feud

VENDETTA is the Italian word for *vengeance.* A VENDETTA is a feud between two families that starts when one family murders someone in the other family. Then the second family murders someone in the first family for revenge. And so it goes on and on, sometimes for generations. The most famous American VENDETTA was between the Hatfields and the McCoys.

"Romeo and Juliet were forbidden to marry because there was a VENDETTA between their families."

"After years of VENDETTA, the two families decided on a truce before they were all wiped out."

Sometimes the word is used in a general sense for any feud that goes on for a long time.

"He had a personal VENDETTA with the company that had sold him the broken typewriter."

DELETE (di-lEt′) v.: to erase, take out, cancel, eliminate

To DELETE something is to take it out, to erase or omit it. The word is usually used about written or printed matter.

"They decided to DELETE this section of the chapter before the book was printed."

"The teacher DELETED Bill's name from the list of those going to the museum."

"I was asked to DELETE that sentence from my speech."

Many people confuse DELETE with *shorten.* To DELETE something is to strike it out entirely, not just to shorten it.

Other forms of the word: DELETION, n.

MIRTH (merth) n.: merriment, laughter, gladness

MIRTH is gladness or happiness accompanied by laughter and fun.

"Everyone was full of MIRTH at the Christmas party."

"They could barely hide their MIRTH as he slipped on a banana peel."

Other forms of the word: MIRTHFUL, adj.
MIRTHLESS, adj.

RABBLE (rab′-əl) n.: a mob, disorderly crowd

A RABBLE is a crowd or mob of people who act stupidly or unthinkingly. The word is always used in an insulting sense.

"He ignored the RABBLE who tried to block his way."

"The RABBLE in the stadium shouted insults at the referee."

A RABBLE-*rouser* is a person who tries to stir up a mob, usually by making speeches.

"Several RABBLE-rousers urged the mob to take the law into its own hands."

Exercise 1

Answer each question with a YES or NO. Put a check in the space for YES or NO next to the question.

	Question	Yes	No
EXAMPLE	Is a speck of dust TINY?	✓	
1.	Does a person have to be old to be SAGE?		
2.	Do policemen usually INDULGE criminals?		
3.	Would most people like to RECTIFY their mistakes?		
4.	Could people be hurt in an INSURRECTION?		
5.	Is it REPREHENSIBLE to be kind to animals?		
6.	Do some people seek SOLACE in eating?		
7.	Would MEMOIRS usually be true?		
8.	Would ten dollars be sufficient RECOMPENSE for someone whose car was stolen?		
9.	Could a face ever be TINGED with sadness?		
10.	Did Germany VANQUISH the United States in World War II?		
11.	Would a thousand-page book be known for its BREVITY?		
12.	Are VENDETTAS generally pleasant?		
13.	Can a single letter be DELETED?		
14.	Does someone who is full of MIRTH need to be cheered up?		
15.	Can RABBLE be dangerous?		

Exercise 2

Each sentence contains a test word in CAPITAL letters. Decide whether the test word is being used correctly or incorrectly in the sentence. Put a check in the space for RIGHT or WRONG next to the sentence.

	Sentence	Right	Wrong
EXAMPLE	After working hard all day Bill felt TINY and wanted to sleep.		✓
1.	Even though we disliked her, we knew she would give us SAGE advice.		
2.	The students INDULGED in all sorts of foolishness when the teacher was away.		
3.	My mother RECTIFIED me for coming home late.		
4.	We worked hard on the INSURRECTION of the newspaper; we wanted to make sure everything was perfect.		
5.	You are old enough now to be REPREHENSIBLE for your own actions.		
6.	It took a great deal of SOLACE to understand what the professor meant.		
7.	In her MEMOIRS she wrote about all the famous people she had met.		

		Right	Wrong
8.	The salesman ran up considerable RECOMPENSES while he was on the road.	____	____
9.	There was a TINGE of anger in his voice when he told them to stop talking.	____	____
10.	The senator VANQUISHED all his opponents in the election.	____	____
11.	I was impressed by the BREVITY with which he could present a complicated argument.	____	____
12.	They waged a political VENDETTA against the senators who had voted against the bill.	____	____
13.	He said that the third clause had to be DELETED before he would sign the contract.	____	____
14.	The actress's silly faces caused some MIRTH in the audience.	____	____
15.	The angry old man said that those teenagers were ignorant RABBLE and should all be locked up.	____	____

Exercise 3

Each test word is followed by three other words. Decide which of the three words is LEAST CLOSELY RELATED in its meaning to the meaning of the test word. Put the letter for the word you choose in the space at the end of the line.

EXAMPLE

	TINY:	a) small	b) short	c) angry	C
1.	SAGE:	a) famous	b) intelligent	c) sensible	____
2.	INDULGE:	a) humor	b) expect	c) spoil	____
3.	RECTIFY:	a) improve	b) repair	c) exchange	____
4.	INSURRECTION:	a) revolt	b) rebel	c) reject	____
5.	REPREHENSIBLE:	a) blameworthy	b) laughable	c) condemnable	____
6.	SOLACE:	a) help	b) relief	c) power	____
7.	MEMOIRS:	a) invention	b) remembrance	c) description	____
8.	RECOMPENSE:	a) accept	b) repay	c) compensate	____
9.	TINGE:	a) shade	b) dirt	c) color	____
10.	VANQUISH:	a) overcome	b) forget	c) conquer	____
11.	BREVITY:	a) quickness	b) fun	c) briefness	____
12.	VENDETTA:	a) despair	b) grudge	c) revenge	____
13.	DELETE:	a) finish	b) remove	c) omit	____
14.	MIRTH:	a) amusement	b) gratefulness	c) happiness	____
15.	RABBLE:	a) crowd	b) audience	c) mob	____

Chapter 9

Pretest

Each test word is printed in CAPITAL letters in a phrase. From the five choices on the next line, select the one which comes nearest in meaning to the meaning of the test word. Underline the one you select.

1. SMUG people.
   insulting · self-satisfied · frightened · clever · funny
2. Known to be VINDICTIVE.
   lying · unkind · vengeful · loving · blameless
3. Continues to BEDEVIL me.
   astound · thrill · torment · defeat · fear
4. NEGLIGIBLE amounts.
   unknown · unimportant · usual · considerable · agreed
5. A very EDIFYING experience.
   shameful · boring · solemn · frightening · uplifting
6. Approached the MALEFACTOR.
   priest · policeman · businessman · criminal · soldier
7. To MUSE on it.
   meditate · sleep · smile · speak · decide
8. To REPROACH them.
   forget · ruin · applaud · meet · blame
9. He sent the ENVOY.
   warning · messenger · spy · guard · ship
10. Found the FISSURE.
    stream · narrow crack · joining place · deep hole · boulder
11. They will COALESCE.
    change · boil · unite · separate · harden
12. After the DELUGE.
    winter · battle · explosion · flood · trick
13. FARCICAL actions.
    violent · serious · unexplained · thoughtless · absurd
14. I SURMISE.
    know · hope · guess · feel · remember
15. They all ASSENTED.
    sat down · finished · prepared · agreed · refused

SMUG (smuhg) adj.: self-satisfied, pleased with oneself, complacent

A SMUG person is quite pleased with himself. SMUG people firmly believe they are right or superior, and take delight in being better than others. SMUGNESS is not a very admirable quality.

"Alice felt quite SMUG after she had beaten her brother at tennis."

"SMUG in his belief that he knew the subject, he didn't bother studying for the test."

"She gave her friends a SMUG smile as she walked up to the stage to receive her award."

Other forms of the word: SMUGNESS, n.

VINDICTIVE (vin-dik'-tiv) adj.: vengeful, unforgiving

VINDICTIVE means "showing a desire for revenge." A VINDICTIVE person by nature wants to get even with anyone who wrongs him.

"She's a VINDICTIVE person. If she thinks you've said something bad about her, she'll spend weeks trying to get back at you."

"My father was stern, but he wasn't VINDICTIVE."

"He made some VINDICTIVE remarks about his old enemy."

"We don't want to be VINDICTIVE; we just want to get back the money he took from us."

BEDEVIL (bi-dev'-əl) v.: to torment, harass, annoy, plague

Be- is a prefix which forms verbs out of nouns. To BEDEVIL someone is to treat him *devilishly,* usually by constantly annoying or worrying him.

"The mosquitoes BEDEVILED us when we camped by the lake."

"This project has been BEDEVILED by problems since the beginning."

"She was BEDEVILED by minor illnesses all year."

In the Pretest, the most commonly chosen incorrect answer is *astound,* perhaps due to a confusion of BEDEVIL with *bedazzle,* which means to *impress forcefully.*

NEGLIGIBLE (neg'-li-jə-bəl) adj.: unimportant, small, not worthy of attention

See *-able* under Suffixes. Anything that is NEGLIGIBLE is able to be neglected without worrying about it, usually because it is so unimportant or tiny.

"The medicine had a NEGLIGIBLE effect. She was no better after taking it than before."

"His attempts to help us were NEGLIGIBLE. I don't think he tried very hard."

"You get a NEGLIGIBLE saving by buying the large economy size. It's just not worth it."

EDIFYING (ed'-ə-fī-ing) adj.: uplifting, enlightening, instructive

EDIFYING and its related verb EDIFY are from the same Latin root as *edifice,* which means "a large and impressive building." To EDIFY originally meant simply to *build.* Now it is only used in the sense of "to build up one's mind or morals."

An "EDIFYING experience" is one which improves you spiritually or intellectually. It is not necessarily an enjoyable experience, although it may be.

"The teacher said it would be an EDIFYING experience for us to go to the museum."

"The minister delivered a very EDIFYING sermon."

Other forms of the word: EDIFY, v.
EDIFICATION, n.

MALEFACTOR (mal'-ə-fak-tər) n.: a criminal, evildoer

MALEFACTOR comes from Latin words meaning "to do evil." A MALEFACTOR is a criminal, or anyone who does evil to another.

"Some unknown MALEFACTOR broke several windows in the school last night."

"The MALEFACTORS must not be allowed to get away with their crime."

The opposite of MALEFACTOR is *benefactor,* someone who does good to other people.

MUSE (myUz) v.: to think, meditate, ponder, reflect

To MUSE *on* or *over* something is to think silently about it. The word usually suggests a dreamy or wondering attitude rather than serious thought.

"He MUSED on the shortness of human life."

"She MUSED over the good times they used to have."

"Sally MUSED about the beauty of nature."

REPROACH (ri-prOch') v.: to blame, criticize, rebuke

To REPROACH someone is to find fault with him, especially in a tone that suggests sorrow or the need for sorrow. The idea is often that of shaming a person into being better.

"Jim's mother REPROACHED him for forgetting her birthday."

"The teacher REPROACHED the students for not studying harder."

REPROACH is also a noun, meaning *blame* or *censure.* A person whose reputation is "above REPROACH" has never done anything he might be blamed for.

"His criminal activities brought REPROACH on his entire family."

Other forms of the word: REPROACHFUL, adj.

ENVOY (on'-voy or en'-voy) n.: a messenger, agent, deputy, representative

ENVOY is from a French word meaning to *send.* An ENVOY is a person sent somewhere as a representative of a government, business, group of people, etc.

"We sent him as our ENVOY to meet with our opponents."

"The ENVOY came to beg us to forgive his king."

In diplomacy, ENVOY is a specific rank of diplomat, second in importance after an ambassader.

Note the different pronunciations. Sometimes words from foreign languages keep their foreign pronunciation for a long time in English. ENVOY seems to be in the process of changing from the French pronunciation on'-voy to the English en'-voy.

FISSURE (fish'-ər) n.: a narrow crack or opening

A FISSURE is a long, narrow crack, usually rather deep, and usually made by splitting or breaking.

"The earthquake caused many FISSURES to appear on the sides of the mountain."

In a broader sense, a FISSURE is a division or disagreement which threatens to break up a group of people.

"A FISSURE developed in the party between those who supported the war and those who opposed it."

"His stand on unemployment opened up many FISSURES in his previously solid support."

COALESCE (kO-ə-les') v.: to unite, join together

To COALESCE is to come or grow together into one body or group. COALESCE often suggests a slow or natural process of growing together.

"Over time the land between them was built up and the two islands finally COALESCED."

"Several small parties managed to COALESCE into one important political organization."

DELUGE (del'-yUj) n.: a flood, downpour

A DELUGE is a great flood, usually caused by a tremendous downpour of rain. A DELUGE can also be anything that overwhelms like a flood.

"When the movie star was sick, the hospital received a DELUGE of mail."

"There was a DELUGE of criticism when the popular teacher was fired."

DELUGE is also a verb meaning to *flood.*

"When the dam broke, towns along the river were DELUGED."

"They DELUGED the company with requests for more information."

"He was DELUGED with job offers after he graduated from schoool."

Battle is the most commonly chosen wrong answer, possibly because DELUGE sometimes has a sense of violence and destructiveness.

FARCICAL (fahr′-sə-kəl or fahr′-si-kəl) adj.: absurd, laughable, ridiculous

A FARCE is a comedy, usually one filled with silly characters and unbelievable situations.

> "We expected a serious drama, but it turned out to be a light-hearted FARCE."

A FARCE is also any situation or event that is like such a comedy.

> "Everything seemed to go wrong; the entire picnic was a complete FARCE."

FARCICAL is the adjective from FARCE. See *-ic* under Suffixes. Something that is FARCICAL is like a FARCE, so silly and extreme that it is funny.

> "His attempts to explain why he was late were almost FARCICAL."
>
> "It was a FARCICAL game. The players seemed to make up the rules as they went along."

Other forms of the word: FARCE, n.

SURMISE (sər-mīz′) v.: to guess, suspect, suppose, think

To SURMISE means "to believe without strong evidence," to *guess* or *suppose.*

> "He SURMISED that there would be a surprise party for him."
>
> "The detective SURMISED that the burglars had entered the house through an open window."

SURMISE is also a noun, which means a *guess.*

> "Her SURMISE proved to be correct."

ASSENT (ə-sent′) v.: to agree, consent, concur

To ASSENT to something is to agree to it. ASSENT often does not suggest strong support but a weaker kind of "going along."

> "My father ASSENTED when I asked him if I could go to the movies."
>
> "I cannot ASSENT to the idea that all men are basically evil."
>
> "Everyone ASSENTED to the proposal that we have a party."

ASSENT is also a noun, meaning *agreement.*

> "The teacher gave her ASSENT to our suggestion that we have a class picnic."

Usage: ASSENT is often followed by *to.*

Exercise 1

Answer each question with a YES or NO. Put a check in the space for YES or NO next to the question.

		Yes	No
EXAMPLE	Is a speck of dust TINY?	✓	
1.	Are SMUG people usually very likable?		
2.	Would a VINDICTIVE person hold a grudge?		
3.	Is it pleasant to be BEDEVILED?		
4.	Would a jackhammer cause a NEGLIGIBLE amount of noise?		
5.	Is an EDIFYING experience always an enjoyable one?		
6.	Can a MALEFACTOR be famous?		
7.	Can you MUSE over something unimportant?		
8.	Do people often feel sorry after they have been REPROACHED?		
9.	Is an ENVOY likely to travel much?		
10.	Is a FISSURE solid?		
11.	Can heat make objects COALESCE?		
12.	Would three letters be a DELUGE of mail?		
13.	Would people be sad at a FARCICAL event?		
14.	Can you SURMISE when you aren't certain?		
15.	Can a person ASSENT to something he doesn't particularly like?		

Exercise 2

Each sentence contains a test word in CAPITAL letters. Decide whether the test word is being used correctly or incorrectly in the sentence. Put a check in the space for RIGHT or WRONG next to the sentence.

		Right	Wrong
EXAMPLE	After working hard all day Bill felt TINY and wanted to sleep.		✓
1.	With a SMUG air of superiority he showed them how to put the puzzle together.		
2.	Our VINDICTIVE neighbors built a large fence just to block our view.		
3.	Doubts about his decision continued to BEDEVIL him long after it had been made.		
4.	Although they worked hard at cleaning the house, the results were NEGLIGIBLE; it was just about as dirty as before.		
5.	She only bought top-quality food to EDIFY her family.		
6.	He had a secret MALEFACTOR who sent him the money to finish college.		
7.	The comedian MUSED us with his jokes.		

		Right	Wrong
8.	The car REPROACHED us at seventy miles an hour.	______	______
9.	The president sent his personal ENVOY to talk with the king.	______	______
10.	The debate over whether to hire him caused a FISSURE in the organization.	______	______
11.	The six streams meet and COALESCE into a river.	______	______
12.	They DELUGED him with prizes after he won the contest.	______	______
13.	His explanation of how electricity works was so obviously wrong it was almost FARCICAL.	______	______
14.	From the way Bill was acting, Mary SURMISED that he was unhappy in his new job.	______	______
15.	She ASSENTED the fact that he made more money than she did for doing the same job.	______	______

Exercise 3

Each test word is followed by three other words. Decide which of the three words is LEAST CLOSELY RELATED in its meaning to the meaning of the test word. Put the letter for the word you choose in the space at the end of the line.

EXAMPLE

	TINY:	a) small	b) short	c) angry	C
1.	SMUG:	a) confident	b) vain	c) eager	______
2.	VINDICTIVE:	a) hopeless	b) merciless	c) spiteful	______
3.	BEDEVIL:	a) trouble	b) annoy	c) defeat	______
4.	NEGLIGIBLE:	a) uncertain	b) insignificant	c) tiny	______
5.	EDIFYING:	a) educational	b) enjoyable	c) uplifting	______
6.	MALEFACTOR:	a) madman	b) thief	c) murderer	______
7.	MUSE:	a) wonder	b) consider	c) discuss	______
8.	REPROACH:	a) scold	b) criticize	c) despise	______
9.	ENVOY:	a) leader	b) diplomat	c) representative	______
10.	FISSURE:	a) split	b) opening	c) increase	______
11.	COALESCE:	a) join	b) add	c) blend	______
12.	DELUGE:	a) overwhelm	b) drown	c) hurt	______
13.	FARCICAL:	a) ridiculous	b) dangerous	c) humorous	______
14.	SURMISE:	a) guess	b) imagine	c) study	______
15.	ASSENT:	a) agree	b) waver	c) comply	______

Review Test 3—Chapters 7–9

Fill in each blank with the test word (or a form of the test word) which best fits the sentence. Use the words listed below.

BAUBLE	DELUGE	INSURRECTION	MUSE	SAGE
BERATE	GIRTH	MALEFACTOR	PARAPHERNALIA	VANQUISH
BREVITY	IMPASSIVE	MEMOIRS	RECTIFY	VENDETTA
DELETE	INSUBORDINATE	MIRTH	REPROACH	VIABLE

1. He always had a(n) ________________ expression on his face. You could never tell what he was thinking.
2. The clerk looked very sad and ________________ the little boy for trying to steal the candy.
3. Because of the huge size of our army we were able to ________________ the enemy in the battle.
4. The police claimed that he was the ________________ responsible for burning down the building.
5. She liked to take a few moments at night, sit by herself, and ________________ over the events of the day.
6. The child was very ________________; she absolutely refused to do what she was told.
7. The company admitted its mistake and promised to ________________ it immediately.
8. His ________________ are full of humorous stories about the events of his life.
9. They were always laughing and joking and full of ________________. It seemed that nothing could make them unhappy.
10. His constant eating increased his ________________ until he couldn't fit into any of his suits.
11. We were amazed by the ________________ of his speech; it only lasted thirty seconds.
12. It is an exciting idea, but it's just not ________________; we would never have enough time to put it into effect.
13. The two families have had a(n) ________________ with each other for generations. By now everyone has forgotten how it started.
14. The policeman angrily ________________ the child for running out into the traffic.
15. The king had to put down several minor ________________ by groups who opposed him.
16. The editor said the book was too long, so he shortened some chapters and ________________ others.
17. They carefully cleaned all the ________________ that would be needed for the job.
18. The tremendous rainstorms caused a(n) ________________ which destroyed many houses.
19. The child quickly grew tired of the bright, pretty ________________ and wanted something more interesting to play with.
20. He is a(n) ________________ and sensible man who is known for his wise handling of difficult problems.

Fill in each blank with the test word (or a form of the test word) which best fits the sentence. Use the words listed below.

ASSENT	DESPOT	GENTEEL	RABBLE	SOLACE
ATTAIN	EDIFYING	INDULGE	REBUKE	SMUG
BEDEVIL	ENVOY	INTERJECTION	RECOMPENSE	SURMISE
COALESCE	FARCICAL	LISTLESS	REPERCUSSION	TINGE
CONSENSUS	FISSURE	NEGLIGIBLE	REPREHENSIBLE	VINDICTIVE

21. There was a slight reddish ____________ to her dress.

22. A series of injuries ____________ the athlete during his playing career.

23. No amount of money could be adequate ____________ for the harm they had done him.

24. It is impossible to ____________ perfection in our work, but we should come as close as we can.

25. I don't think what she did was so ____________; I wouldn't criticize anyone for just trying to tell the truth.

26. The principal gave a very ____________ speech on the importance of studying. We all learned a lot.

27. The police were instructed to keep the ____________ off the streets so that the visiting king would see only clean, respectful tradespeople.

28. Jim's mother ____________ him strongly for not obeying her.

29. Al feels very ____________ sometimes. He just wants to sleep and eat and watch television.

30. I'm not sure exactly when he'll be back, but I ____________ that he'll be here in time for supper.

31. The ____________ of the committee was that it needed more time before it could reach a final decision.

32. Some of the poison leaked out, but the amount was ____________; it wasn't enough to harm anyone.

33. We sent our ____________ to the new country to tell them of our peaceful intentions.

34. The clown's ____________ attempt to ride a bicycle backward had everyone laughing.

35. Both of us ____________ to the arrangement by which we split the reward equally.

36. The war between the two little countries had serious ____________ throughout the world.

37. The climber fell into the deep ____________ in the side of the mountain.

38. Art wasn't ____________ when people wronged him; he didn't believe in seeking revenge.

39. The parents ____________ their children by letting them stay up an extra hour.

40. He lived in ____________ poverty. He wore the most expensive suits, but they were threadbare and ragged.

41. He was quite ____________ about his victory, and said the losers would never be as good as he was.

42. Several small groups of people ____________ into one large crowd.

43. As he grew older the king became more and more of a(n) ____________, making all laws by himself and jailing anyone who opposed him.

44. Many kind friends came to offer ____________ to her in her time of trouble.

45. She shouted out "Wonderful!", "Marvelous!", and other ____________ during the exciting concert.

Chapter 10

Pretest

Each test word is printed in CAPITAL letters in a phrase. From the five choices on the next line, select the one which comes nearest in meaning to the meaning of the test word. Underline the one you select.

1.	His EMPHATIC reply.				
	mild	forceful	quick	insulting	puzzling
2.	Its INCEPTION.				
	improvement	end	beginning	approval	value
3.	GINGERLY movements.				
	silent	clumsy	careful	slow	quick
4.	Bronze IMPLEMENT.				
	cup	decoration	weapon	statue	tool
5.	To PALPITATE continuously.				
	bother	work	worry	throb	float
6.	INTREPID men.				
	brilliant	fearless	cowardly	cold	watchful
7.	Visited the MATRON.				
	married woman	young girl	bride	rich man	teacher
8.	PALATABLE food.				
	unsurpassed	sweet	tasty	disagreeable	colorless
9.	Unusually RETICENT.				
	frightened	sad	quiet	lonely	noisy
10.	SORDID surroundings.				
	dangerous	filthy	magnificent	ruined	various
11.	DISCREET refusal.				
	secret	tactful	proud	total	thoughtless
12.	She felt AGGRIEVED.				
	relaxed	neglected	satisfied	tired	wronged
13.	The EQUITY of the decision.				
	purpose	acceptance	fairness	importance	result
14.	A small LEGACY.				
	association	request	inheritance	profit	mistake
15.	Considered them PLEBEIAN.				
	clumsy	majestic	holy	commonplace	foreign

EMPHATIC (em-fat′-ik) adj.: forceful, insistent, strongly expressive, striking

EMPHASIS is the stress or force used to show that something is important.

> "The coach laid great EMPHASIS on speed."

EMPHATIC is the adjective from EMPHASIS. See *-ic* under Suffixes. EMPHATIC means *forceful, insistent.*

> "The mayor issued an EMPHATIC denial to the rumor that he was seriously ill."
> "Jim's tone was EMPHATIC when he said he would never let Bill drive his car again."
> "The teacher said EMPHATICALLY that there would be absolutely no talking during the test."

Other forms of the word: EMPHASIS, n.
EMPHASIZE, v.

INCEPTION (in-sep′-shən) n.: beginning, start, commencement

INCEPTION is a rather formal word for the *beginning* or *start* of something. The word is used especially about projects, organizations, practices, and the like.

> "Since the INCEPTION of the fund-raising drive we have received over ten thousand dollars."
> "I was present at the club's INCEPTION two years ago."
> "The plot of the novel changed greatly between the book's INCEPTION and its completion."

GINGERLY (jin′-jər-lE) adj.: careful, cautious, wary

GINGERLY means *careful* or *cautious.* To do something in a GINGERLY manner is to do it with care, in order to avoid hurting yourself, making a noise, or breaking something.

> "They moved in a GINGERLY way across the beach, looking out for pieces of broken glass."

GINGERLY is also an adverb.

> "He GINGERLY picked up the priceless vase and carried it across the room."
> "We walked GINGERLY through the minefield, afraid that any second we would be blown up."

IMPLEMENT (im′-plə-mənt) n.: a tool, instrument

An IMPLEMENT is a *tool,* an object used in carrying out some kind of work.

> "She had a hoe, a rake, and other gardening IMPLEMENTS."
> "As part of the peace treaty they agreed to give up all their IMPLEMENTS of war."
> "Television can be used as an IMPLEMENT of education."

IMPLEMENT is also a verb (pronounced im′-plə-ment), meaning to *carry out* or *put into effect.*

> "The workers were told to IMPLEMENT the president's new policy immediately."
> "It's easy to make a decision; it's more difficult to IMPLEMENT it."

In the Pretest, the most popular wrong answer is *decoration.* This may be due to a confusion between IMPLEMENT and *ornament,* which is a *decoration.*

Other forms of the word: IMPLEMENTATION, n.

PALPITATE (pal′-pə-tAt) v.: to throb, beat rapidly, pulsate, quiver

To PALPITATE is to beat rapidly and strongly, like the heart during exercise or strong emotion.

> "Her heart started to PALPITATE whenever she thought of the man she loved."
> "Running up the flight of stairs caused the man's heart to PALPITATE."

Other forms of the word: PALPITATION, n.

INTREPID (in-trep′-id) adj.: fearless, daring, brave

See $in\text{-}_2$ under Prefixes. The *trepid* part of the word comes from a Latin word meaning *fear,* also the source of the English word *trepidation.* Someone who is INTREPID is *fearless;* he is daring and resolute when it comes to meeting danger.

> "The INTREPID explorers set off into the jungle, knowing they might never come out alive."

Other forms of the word: INTREPIDITY, n.

MATRON (mA′-trən) n.: a dignified married woman

A MATRON is a married woman, especially a mature or dignified one with a high social position.

> "They were dignified old MATRONS who spent most of their time on the committees for various charities."

MATRON is also used for the woman who is in charge of the housekeeping at a hospital, prison, or similar institution.

Other forms of the word: MATRONLY, adj.

PALATABLE (pal′-ət-ə-bəl) adj.: tasty, agreeable to the taste

See *-able* under Suffixes. The *palate* is the roof of the mouth; it was once popularly thought to be where the sense of taste was located. Thus, something which is PALATABLE is agreeable to the *palate* or the taste. The word is usually used about foods that are little more than acceptable to the palate, and not about foods which taste wonderful.

> "The dinner he cooked was at least PALATABLE, which is more than I expected."
>
> "This vegetable can be PALATABLE if it is cooked the right way."

Sometimes PALATABLE is used in a general sense to mean *agreeable, acceptable.*

> "You may not find my criticisms very PALATABLE, but I'm still going to make them."

RETICENT (ret′-ə-sənt) adj.: silent, reserved, quiet

Someone who is RETICENT is not inclined to say much, either out of caution or shyness. A RETICENT person keeps most things to himself, and only gives out information grudgingly.

> "She was RETICENT about what had happened that day. It was obvious she was hiding something."
>
> "He is usually RETICENT about all his accomplishments, but this time he told everyone."
>
> "Don't be RETICENT. Let us know how you feel."

Other forms of the word: RETICENCE, n.

SORDID (sôr′-did) adj.: filthy, dirty

Someone or something that is SORDID is filthy and disgusting. The word's basic meaning is *dirty,* but it always suggests uncleanness that is caused by evil or corruption.

> "It was difficult for children to grow up in these SORDID surroundings."
>
> "He had some SORDID habits which caused all decent people to avoid him."
>
> "The evil criminals carried out their SORDID plot to kidnap the child."

DISCREET (dis-krEt′) adj.: tactful, cautious, careful

A person who is DISCREET shows good judgment in what he says or does. He is very careful not to do anything which might harm his own interests or those of his friends. A DISCREET person can be trusted with a secret, or with a task that requires tact and diplomacy.

> "The DISCREET diplomat refused to criticize the leaders of the foreign country."
>
> "She thought it would be DISCREET to leave before the party got too wild."

A "DISCREET silence" occurs when someone has decided that it's better not to say anything in a particular situation.

Other forms of the word: DISCRETION, n.
DISCRETIONARY, adj.

AGGRIEVED (ə-grEvd′) adj.: wronged, offended, troubled

AGGRIEVED is related to the words *grief* and *grieve.* To be AGGRIEVED is to be wronged or treated unjustly, so that you have cause for complaint.

> "He felt AGGRIEVED when the teacher punished him and not the rest of the students."
>
> "Bill had a permanently AGGRIEVED attitude; he thought that people were always treating him badly."

The most commonly chosen wrong answer is *neglected.* Someone who is *neglected* may have a right to feel AGGRIEVED, but the two words do not have the same meaning.

Other forms of the word: AGGRIEVE, v.

EQUITY (ek'-wə-tE) n.: fairness, impartiality, justice

EQUITY is related to the word *equal.* EQUITY is the quality of being fair, just, and impartial.

> "The EQUITY of his solution seemed to please everyone."
>
> "He thought that as a matter of EQUITY he should get a share."

In English and American law, EQUITY is a particular system of rules and doctrines which is designed to correct or override other laws in cases where they appear to work unfairly.

The adjective formed from EQUITY is EQUITABLE, which means *reasonable, just.*

> "It was hardly an EQUITABLE arrangement, since she paid for the car and he was the only one who could use it."

Other forms of the word: EQUITABLE, adj.

LEGACY (leg'-ə-sE) n.: an inheritance, bequest

A LEGACY is something, like land or money, left by will as a gift to someone else.

> "Her uncle left her a small LEGACY which helped pay for her college education."

In a general sense, a LEGACY is anything received from the past or from our ancestors.

> "Their chief LEGACY to their children was a keen desire to help the unfortunate."
>
> "Those beautiful paintings are our LEGACY from the great artists of the past."

PLEBEIAN (plə-bE'-ən) adj.: commonplace, undistinguished

In ancient Rome there were two classes of people, the *plebs,* or common people, and the *patricians,* or nobles. The adjective PLEBEIAN means "of or relating to the *plebs* or common people." The word is used about people, things, or activities that are considered crude or commonplace.

> "The nobleman didn't want his daughter to marry into such a PLEBEIAN family."
>
> "He considered himself too cultured to take part in so PLEBEIAN a sport as bowling."

PLEBEIAN is also a noun.

> "I may only be a simple PLEBEIAN, but I have rights too."

Exercise 1

Answer each question with a YES or NO. Put a check in the space for YES or NO next to each question.

	Yes	No
EXAMPLE Is a speck of dust TINY?	✓	
1. If a teacher puts EMPHASIS on neatness, does she care about it?		
2. Has a project gotten very far at the time of its INCEPTION?		
3. If someone had to carry a bomb, would he carry it GINGERLY?		
4. Could a pen be considered an IMPLEMENT?		
5. Is a heart always PALPITATING?		
6. Are mountain climbers usually INTREPID?		
7. Can a baby be a MATRON?		
8. Is dirt PALATABLE?		
9. Would most salesmen be RETICENT?		
10. Can a person be SORDID?		
11. Should a secret agent be DISCREET?		
12. Is a person who feels AGGRIEVED likely to be angry at someone?		
13. Should people be angry about an EQUITABLE decision?		
14. Could a diamond ring be a LEGACY?		
15. Would a duchess be a PLEBEIAN?		

Exercise 2

Each sentence contains a test word in CAPITAL letters. Decide whether the test word is being used correctly or incorrectly in the sentence. Put a check in the space for RIGHT or WRONG next to the sentence.

	Right	Wrong
EXAMPLE After working hard all day Bill felt TINY and wanted to sleep.		✓
1. He struck the table EMPHATICALLY to show that he meant what he said.		
2. The school held an INCEPTION so that everyone could meet the new principal.		
3. They GINGERLY picked up the child and placed her in the ambulance.		
4. They IMPLEMENTED the actor on his fine performance.		
5. He PALPITATED the switch to make sure it worked.		
6. He was so INTREPID that his hand started to shake as he opened the door.		
7. His grandmother was a distinguished MATRON.		
8. I expected a wonderful meal; instead I got some stale bread that was barely PALATABLE.		

		Right	Wrong
9.	The RETICENT boy wouldn't tell his parents why he was afraid to go to school.	✓	
10.	Everyone admired the SORDID way he treated his children.		✓
11.	When asked if she would run for reelection, the senator kept a DISCREET silence.	✓	
12.	Her AGGRIEVED expression showed that she was feeling sorry for herself again.	✓	
13.	We were amazed by the EQUITY of the arrangement, under which she got less pay for the same amount of work.		✓
14.	A continuing hostility between the two countries was the unfortunate LEGACY of the ancient war.	✓	
15.	She felt that watching television was a PLEBEIAN activity, and refused to do it.	✓	

Exercise 3

Each test word is followed by three other words. Decide which of the three words is LEAST CLOSELY RELATED in its meaning to the meaning of the test word. Put the letter for the word you choose in the space at the end of the line.

EXAMPLE

	TINY:	**a)** small	**b)** short	**c)** angry	C
1.	EMPHATIC:	**a)** cruel	**b)** strong	**c)** insistent	A
2.	INCEPTION:	**a)** origin	**b)** victory	**c)** start	B
3.	GINGERLY:	**a)** cautiously	**b)** worriedly	**c)** accurately	B [C]
4.	IMPLEMENT:	**a)** road	**b)** device	**c)** machine	A
5.	PALPITATE:	**a)** vibrate	**b)** tremble	**c)** ache	A [C]
6.	INTREPID:	**a)** bold	**b)** rude	**c)** daring	B
7.	MATRON:	**a)** elderly	**b)** ill	**c)** dignified	B
8.	PALATABLE:	**a)** possible	**b)** edible	**c)** acceptable	A
9.	RETICENT:	**a)** shy	**b)** secretive	**c)** sad	C
10.	SORDID:	**a)** expensive	**b)** mean	**c)** vile	A
11.	DISCREET:	**a)** happy	**b)** quiet	**c)** careful	A
12.	AGGRIEVED:	**a)** upset	**b)** offended	**c)** nervous	C
13.	EQUITY:	**a)** justness	**b)** fairness	**c)** brilliance	C
14.	LEGACY:	**a)** earnings	**b)** inheritance	**c)** gift	A
15.	PLEBEIAN:	**a)** easy	**b)** average	**c)** common	A

Chapter 11

Pretest

Each test word is printed in CAPITAL letters in a phrase. From the five choices on the next line, select the one which comes nearest in meaning to the meaning of the test word. Underline the one you select.

1. RECAPITULATE the argument.
   continue — answer — sum up — end — lose
2. The EXODUS began.
   prayer — mass departure — trip — long visit — miracle
3. The guests IMBIBED.
   ate — were late — wrote — stayed sober — drank
4. To HEW it.
   replace — cut — burn — fix — kill
5. ILLUSTRIOUS men.
   famous — happy — beloved — unknown — hardworking
6. WANTON people.
   needy — immoral — rare — popular — holy
7. To IMPART knowledge.
   lose — hide — divide up — gain — make known
8. Full of WILES.
   smiles — danger — fear — tears — tricks
9. He ESPOUSES their plan.
   admires — requests — opposes — supports — demands
10. Carefully WROUGHT.
    shaped — colored — placed — chosen — purchased
11. LAUDABLE actions.
    impossible — praiseworthy — silly — understandable — clever
12. He was CULPABLE.
    miserable — wonderful — evil — effective — blameworthy
13. Several PICAYUNE points.
    typical — boring — trivial — crucial — different
14. SCATHING reports.
    revealing — exciting — disturbing — damaging — disagreeing
15. SUPERFICIAL treatment.
    formal — unnecessary — shallow — careful — mistaken

RECAPITULATE (rE-kə-pich'-ə-lAt) v.: to sum up, summarize, restate briefly

To RECAPITULATE means to *sum up* an argument, a discussion, or the like, by going over the main points again.

"At the end of the debate both sides briefly RECAPITULATED their positions."

"She RECAPITULATED the reasons why she should be elected president."

"I would like to RECAPITULATE what other writers have said about this novel."

In the Pretest, many people choose *continue* as the meaning of RECAPITULATE, but RECAPITULATE means to *summarize,* usually with a view towards ending a speech or an argument.

Other forms of the word: RECAPITULATION, n.

EXODUS (ek'-sə-dəs) n.: a mass departure, emigration

The EXODUS was the departure of the Israelites from Egypt, described in the second book of the Bible. An EXODUS has come to mean any departure or going away of a large group of people, with or without the difficulties that the Israelites had in leaving Egypt. See *ex-* under Prefixes.

"The promise of better jobs in the growing cities caused a large EXODUS of workers from rural areas."

The most popular wrong answer is *trip,* which is close to the meaning of EXODUS but not quite the same. One person could go by himself on a *trip* to the store, but this would not be an EXODUS.

IMBIBE (im-bIb') v.: to drink, drink in, absorb

IMBIBE comes from Latin words meaning "to drink in." See *in-*$_1$ under Prefixes. The word means actual drinking and "drinking in" or absorbing ideas, knowledge, and the like.

"He tried to IMBIBE all the knowledge the teacher could give him."

When IMBIBE means actual drinking, it sometimes has a rather humorous tone.

"The drunk said he only IMBIBED on national holidays."

HEW (hyU) v.: to cut, chop, carve

To HEW something is to cut it. The word usually suggests a rough job of cutting, done with an ax, a sword, or the like.

"He HEWED the trunk of the tree with one mighty blow of his ax."

"This statue was HEWN out of solid rock."

"They had to HEW a path for themselves through the thick jungle."

"She HEWED the branches from the tree."

Usage: The past participle of HEW is HEWN.

ILLUSTRIOUS (i-luhs'-trE-əs) adj.: famous, eminent, distinguished, celebrated

ILLUSTRIOUS comes from a Latin word meaning to *brighten,* also the source of the word *luster.* People who are ILLUSTRIOUS are famous. They are brilliantly distinguished because of what they have done or because of their good qualities.

"Our ILLUSTRIOUS ancestors made this nation as great as it is today."

"This novel will make the ILLUSTRIOUS writer even more famous."

"When the ILLUSTRIOUS judge retired, everyone honored him for his wisdom and mercy."

Hardworking is the most commonly chosen incorrect answer, probably because of confusion between ILLUSTRIOUS and *industrious.*

WANTON (won'-tən) adj.: immoral, irresponsible, reckless, undisciplined

The basic meaning of WANTON is "lacking discipline." The word is used in several ways using this idea. WANTON can mean "done unjustifiably," *malicious.*

"The youths were charged with the WANTON attack on the old man."

It can mean *extravagant, unchecked.*

"Your WANTON spending is going to make us all poor."

Or it can mean *immoral, unchaste.*

"These WANTON people are a disgrace to the neighborhood."

Rare is the most commonly chosen wrong answer, perhaps because of the *want* part of the word.

IMPART (im-pahrt′) v.: to make known, communicate, transmit, pass on

To IMPART means to *communicate,* to *pass on.* The word is used in two different senses. The first is to *give* or *pass on* a quality or condition to something.

"The new carpet IMPARTED a certain elegance to the dining room."

"The general's signature at the bottom IMPARTED a great deal of authority to the orders."

The second sense is simply to *tell* or *make known* something.

"I want to IMPART some secret information to you."

"The professor IMPARTED his knowledge to the students."

WILE (wīl) n.: a trick, ploy, ruse

A WILE is a trick used to entrap someone or to lure him on.

"The babysitter had to use all her WILES to get the children to go to bed."

"He was not taken in by her WILES, and refused to go along with the scheme."

"We used all our WILES, but we still couldn't get the teacher to postpone the test."

WILY is the adjective from WILE. See *-y* under Suffixes. WILY means *tricky, crafty, sly.*

"The WILY old thief knew all the ways to steal people's money."

Usage: WILE is usually used in the plural, WILES.

ESPOUSE (es-powz′ or es-pows′) v.: to support, adopt, make one's own, come to believe in

A *spouse* is a marriage partner, a husband or wife. To ESPOUSE meant originally "to take as a spouse," to *wed.* The word is still sometimes used in this way, but it usually now has the sense "to attach yourself to a cause or a belief" as if you were married to it.

"They eagerly ESPOUSED the doctrine of equal pay for equal work."

"Everyone ESPOUSED the miners' cause."

"He ESPOUSED a strange theory that turned out to be correct."

ESPOUSE is a stronger word than *believe* or *support*; it suggests more eagerness and completeness in your feelings.

"Once he had ESPOUSED this new idea, no one could talk him out of it."

WROUGHT (rôt) adj.: shaped, fashioned, formed

WROUGHT is an old form of the past tense of *work.* WROUGHT as an adjective basically means *worked.* The word is usually applied to objects that have been carefully or elaborately fashioned, especially by hand.

"He bought his wife a pair of beautifully WROUGHT earrings for her birthday."

"The lovely hand-WROUGHT lampshade was quite expensive."

When used of metals, WROUGHT means "beaten or hammered into shape with tools."

"The candlesticks were WROUGHT of the finest silver."

In a different sense WROUGHT is used in the phrase "WROUGHT up," which means *worked up, excited.*

"My mother gets all WROUGHT up when I don't come home on time."

LAUDABLE (lôd′-ə-bəl) adj.: praiseworthy, deserving praise, commendable

See *-able* under Suffixes. LAUD is a rare word meaning to *praise highly.* Something or someone that is LAUDABLE is able to be praised, is worthy of being praised.

"Your desire to increase your vocabulary is LAUDABLE."

"We thought his opinions were LAUDABLE, but we didn't like the way he insisted that everyone agree with him."

Understandable is the most commonly chosen wrong answer, perhaps because LAUDABLE sounds like *audible,* which means "able to be heard."

CULPABLE (kuhl′-pə-bəl) adj.: blameworthy

See *-able* under Suffixes. The *culp* part of the word comes from a Latin word meaning *blame,* also the source of the word *culprit.* Someone or something that is CULPABLE is worthy of being blamed for something, deserves condemnation or punishment.

"The judge said her parents were as CULPABLE for her crimes as she was."

"You cannot consider him CULPABLE, since he was forced to do what he did."

"His ignorance of the dangerous situation was CULPABLE, because it was his job to know about such things."

The most commonly chosen incorrect answer is *effective,* probably because of a confusion between CULPABLE and *capable.*

Other forms of the word: CULPABILITY, n.

PICAYUNE (pik′-E-yUn or pik′-ə-yUn) adj.: trivial, trifling, small, unworthy of notice

A PICAYUNE was a small coin used in the Spanish colonies in America. When the Americans took over the word, it came to be used as an adjective which means *small, insignificant, practically worthless.*

"She owes a PICAYUNE amount—not more than a dollar."

"Several of the patients had PICAYUNE complaints about their treatment, but everyone was pleased in general."

"He thought her criticisms were PICAYUNE; they were just about minor points that didn't make any difference."

SCATHING (skATH′-ing) adj.: damaging, harmful, very severe

SCATHING is an old English word which meant *harmful, damaging,* or *injurious.* SCATHING is now used chiefly about damaging or harmful words.

"The reviewer gave a SCATHING criticism of the new play, saying that the author couldn't write and that the actors couldn't perform."

"The boss's SCATHING reply to Ken's suggestion hurt him deeply."

The related word UNSCATHED means *unharmed, undamaged.*

"It was a miracle she walked away from the accident UNSCATHED."

Other forms of the word: UNSCATHED, adj.

SUPERFICIAL (sU-pər-fish′-əl) adj.: shallow, trivial, insignificant

SUPERFICIAL comes from the Latin word for *surface.* Something which is SUPERFICIAL is on the surface only; it doesn't go very deep. A SUPERFICIAL wound is a minor wound which just involves the surface of the skin. When applied to people and their actions, SUPERFICIAL means "concerned only with what is on the surface, with what is apparent and obvious."

"It was a SUPERFICIAL report. It just gave the facts, not the reasons behind them."

"The doctor gave him a quick, SUPERFICIAL examination and said he was all right."

Other forms of the word: SUPERFICIALITY, n.

Exercise 1

Answer each question with a YES or NO. Put a check in the space for YES or NO next to each question.

	Yes	No
EXAMPLE Is a speck of dust TINY?	✓	____
1. Can you RECAPITULATE what someone else has said?	____	____
2. Is it an EXODUS when a person leaves his house in the morning?	____	____
3. Can you IMBIBE milk?	____	____
4. Can you HEW a table?	____	____
5. Is Adolf Hitler ILLUSTRIOUS?	____	____
6. Are WANTON people always poor?	____	____
7. Do dictionaries IMPART information?	____	____
8. Would it be easy to cheat a WILY person?	____	____
9. Do people who are against change ESPOUSE it?	____	____
10. Would a highly WROUGHT piece of furniture usually be plain?	____	____
11. Is it LAUDABLE to save a person from drowning?	____	____
12. Would a person be CULPABLE if he struck a car while driving on the wrong side of the road?	____	____
13. Is PICAYUNE criticism helpful to a person?	____	____
14. Do mothers sing SCATHING lullabies to their babies?	____	____
15. Would a SUPERFICIAL injury usually be very serious?	____	____

Exercise 2

Each sentence contains a test word in CAPITAL letters. Decide whether the test word is being used correctly or incorrectly in the sentence. Put a check in the space for RIGHT or WRONG next to the sentence.

	Right	Wrong
EXAMPLE After working hard all day Bill felt TINY and wanted to sleep.	____	✓
1. Hal RECAPITULATED his main arguments against the proposal.	____	____
2. The governor tried to stop the EXODUS of businesses from his state by lowering taxes.	____	____
3. He IMBIBED her not to give in.	____	____
4. An immense hole was HEWN in the side of the mountain.	____	____
5. The ILLUSTRIOUS composer wrote some of the greatest symphonies of our time.	____	____
6. The judge criticized their WANTON disregard for the ordinary standards of decency.	____	____

		Right	Wrong
7.	His presence IMPARTED a sense of importance to the meeting.		
8.	He knew about all his opponent's WILES and didn't let himself be trapped.		
9.	All the students ESPOUSED the idea of a shorter school day.		
10.	The robbers took all his money and then WROUGHT him up.		
11.	His first attempt at playing the trumpet was LAUDABLE. No one could stay in the same room when he was practicing.		
12.	John is our most CULPABLE salesman; no one is as good as he is.		
13.	You had better not make a mistake. This is the most PICAYUNE decision you will ever have to make.		
14.	Many were injured in the explosion, but Barry was UNSCATHED.		
15.	That movie was SUPERFICIAL. I think it's the best I've ever seen.		

Exercise 3

Each test word is followed by three other words. Decide which of the three words is LEAST CLOSELY RELATED in its meaning to the meaning of the test word. Put the letter for the word you choose in the space at the end of the line.

EXAMPLE

		a)	b)	c)	
	TINY:	a) small	b) short	c) angry	C
1.	RECAPITULATE:	a) explain	b) repeat	c) summarize	
2.	EXODUS:	a) emigration	b) departure	c) visit	
3.	IMBIBE:	a) absorb	b) drink	c) eat	
4.	HEW:	a) spill	b) split	c) saw	
5.	ILLUSTRIOUS:	a) different	b) great	c) distinguished	
6.	WANTON:	a) extravagant	b) powerful	c) spiteful	
7.	IMPART:	a) know	b) tell	c) transmit	
8.	WILE:	a) cheat	b) winner	c) fake	
9.	ESPOUSE:	a) applaud	b) believe	c) erect	
10.	WROUGHT:	a) fixed	b) made	c) formed	
11.	LAUDABLE:	a) good	b) rare	c) worthwhile	
12.	CULPABLE:	a) guilty	b) unreasonable	c) responsible	
13.	PICAYUNE:	a) petty	b) lost	c) worthless	
14.	SCATHING:	a) bitter	b) ridiculous	c) insulting	
15.	SUPERFICIAL:	a) outward	b) insignificant	c) extraordinary	

Chapter 12

Pretest

Each test word is printed in CAPITAL letters in a phrase. From the five choices on the next line, select the one which comes nearest in meaning to the meaning of the test word. Underline the one you select.

1. Remarkable AFFINITY.
   concern — distrust — attraction — history — distance
2. Amazing VISTA.
   area — future — view — times — idea
3. ASPIRE to be the leader.
   demand — ask — long — claim — refuse
4. Completely ASSIMILATED.
   rejected — hidden — absorbed — recognized — revealed
5. The IMPETUS behind it.
   rushing around — happiness — thought — moving force — indifference
6. ARDENT desire.
   new — real — constant — burning — mild
7. He will CONFOUND anyone.
   anger — please — discover — impress — confuse
8. REVEL until dawn.
   sleep — make merry — fight — sing — work hard
9. BESTIAL behavior.
   criminal — excellent — animal-like — logical — unusual
10. Forget about the ORDEAL.
    triumph — contract — accident — severe trial — strange sight
11. AFFABLE men.
    stupid — vicious — competent — pleasant — holy
12. BLASÉ expression.
    indifferent — lively — sulky — innocent — old-fashioned
13. To DEFILE it.
    hate — clean — steal — dirty — break
14. BANAL ideas.
    mistaken — unique — annoying — fashionable — commonplace
15. He was EXONERATED.
    accused — cleared — found guilty — released — arrested

AFFINITY (ə-fin′-ə-tE) n.: an attraction, natural liking, close connection

An AFFINITY *for* something is a strong liking for or attraction to it.

"She found she had an AFFINITY for speaking in public."

"They felt a strange AFFINITY for the deserted old house."

An AFFINITY *with* or *between* things or people is a close resemblance or connection between them.

"There is a strong AFFINITY between the two writers."

"The English language has many AFFINITIES with German."

AFFINITY has some very specific uses involving this basic idea of *attraction* or *connection.* AFFINITY is relationship by marriage (as opposed to a relationship by blood). In chemistry, AFFINITY is the force by which atoms are held together in chemical compounds.

VISTA (vis′-tə) n.: a view, prospect

A VISTA is a *view,* especially one seen through or along a narrow passage or avenue.

"We saw the beautiful VISTA of the distant mountains through the long rows of trees."

"A VISTA of the huge mansion appeared to them at the end of the driveway."

A VISTA can also be a mental view extending over long periods of time or many matters.

"Einstein's theories opened many new VISTAS for research in physics."

ASPIRE (ə-spIr′) v.: to long, yearn, be ambitious

To ASPIRE *to* or *after* something is to be filled with ambition to reach it or accomplish it. You usually ASPIRE to something grand or important.

"Jane ASPIRED to the presidency."

"She ASPIRED to be the best singer of her time."

"Tom only ASPIRED after knowledge; nothing else mattered to him."

ASPIRATION is the noun from ASPIRE and means *ambition, goal.*

"His one ASPIRATION is to be a professional baseball player."

Other forms of the word: ASPIRATION, n.

ASSIMILATE (ə-sim′-ə-lAt) v.: to absorb, take in

To ASSIMILATE something is to take it in so that it becomes a part of you. The word can be used about food.

"The body can ASSIMILATE some foods more easily than others."

Or it can be used in a wider sense of ideas or knowledge.

"Johnny found it difficult to ASSIMILATE all the material the teacher presented to the class."

The word is also used about races and cultural groups.

"It took many years before the immigrants were completely ASSIMILATED into American society."

Other forms of the word: ASSIMILATION, n.

IMPETUS (im′-pə-təs) n.: a moving force, impulse, stimulus

IMPETUS is the force behind something, the energy with which it is moving.

"He gave the tricycle a push, and this IMPETUS carried it all the way down the street."

"The train didn't have enough IMPETUS to get to the top of the hill."

IMPETUS is also used in a more general sense to mean any *driving force* or *stimulus.*

"The idea of getting rich quick was a strong IMPETUS behind the gold rush."

"His enthusiasm was the real IMPETUS behind the project."

ARDENT (ahr′-dənt) adj.: burning, warm, passionate, enthusiastic

ARDENT comes from a Latin word meaning to *burn.* ARDENT is now not often used about actual fire or heat, but means *on fire* with desire, enthusiasm, or some other strong emotion.

"He was an ARDENT supporter of free speech."

"She felt an ARDENT desire to see her native land once more."

"He spoke ARDENTLY of his love for his wife."

The noun related to ARDENT is ARDOR, which means "warmth of emotion," *passion, zeal.*

"His ARDOR for chess cooled when he started playing opponents who could beat him."

Other forms of the word: ARDOR, n.

CONFOUND (kən-fownd′ or kahn-fownd′) v.: to confuse, mix up, puzzle, perplex

CONFOUND comes from Latin words which mean to *pour together.* See *con-* under Prefixes. To CONFOUND things is to mix them up so that one thing is confused with another.

"The author's error is to CONFOUND the desire to do good with the good deed itself."

To CONFOUND a person is to confuse him. CONFOUND in this sense is a rather strong word, and suggests such total puzzlement that it is difficult for a person to act.

"The sudden disappearance of the jewels CONFOUNDED everyone."

"They were CONFOUNDED by his stubborn refusal to go along."

In the Pretest, many people choose *anger* as the meaning of CONFOUND, probably because CONFOUND is used in a mild oath, "CONFOUND it." In this sense, CONFOUND means *damn.* It is an expression of anger, but it doesn't mean to make someone angry.

REVEL (rev′-əl) v.: to make merry

To REVEL is to make merry, to be festive.

"They REVELED for days when they heard the war was over."

To REVEL *in* something is take great delight in it.

"He seemed to REVEL in making people feel uncomfortable."

"They REVELED in their freedom when school was over."

REVEL is also a noun meaning *merrymaking, noisy festivities.*

"It was quite a REVEL. The fun lasted until dawn."

"There were REVELS every night on the millionaire's yacht."

Other forms of the word: REVELRY, n.

BESTIAL (bes′-chəl or bEs′-chəl) adj.: beast-like, brutal, savage

BESTIAL is an adjective from *beast.* See *-al* under Suffixes. The word means "of or like a beast" and usually emphasizes the cruelty and savagery of a wild animal.

"The BESTIAL soldiers killed the women and children in cold blood."

"They should go to prison for life for their BESTIAL crimes."

"His BESTIAL behavior when he has been drinking shocks everyone."

The noun from BESTIAL is BESTIALITY, which is the quality of being a beast.

"The BESTIALITY of these vicious criminals outraged the public."

Other forms of the word: BESTIALITY, n.

ORDEAL (ôr-dEl′) n.: a severe trial

In ancient times, one way of deciding whether a person was guilty or innocent of a crime was to make the person undergo a severe or painful test like walking through fire. If the person survived this test, he was thought to be innocent of the crime. This test was known as an ORDEAL.

Nowadays, ORDEAL is used for any severe test or trying experience.

"Being lost in the desert without water was quite an ORDEAL."

"For her, every math test was an ORDEAL."

"It was a terrible ORDEAL for him to speak before a crowd."

AFFABLE (af′-ə-bəl) adj.: pleasant, friendly, gracious

See *-able* under Suffixes. AFFABLE comes from Latin words meaning "able to speak to." An AFFABLE person is easy to talk to; he is friendly and polite to everyone.

"The manager was unusually AFFABLE this morning; she laughed and joked with everyone on the staff."

"Our boss is very AFFABLE; he even stops and says hello to the part-time clerks."

Competent is the most commonly chosen wrong answer. Perhaps the people who choose this are confused by the *-able* part of AFFABLE and think the word means *capable.*

Other forms of the word: AFFABILITY, n.

BLASÉ (blah-zA′) adj.: indifferent, world-weary

BLASÉ is a French word, and keeps its French pronunciation.

A BLASÉ person has experienced so many pleasures (or pretends that he has) that he has become bored with them. The things that excite or interest the average person leave him indifferent and unimpressed.

> "She was quite BLASÉ about winning the prize. You'd think it happened to her every day."
>
> "With a BLASÉ shrug of his shoulders he said it didn't matter to him whether he went on the trip or not."
>
> "He tried to act BLASÉ about being elected class president, but he couldn't hide his excitement."

Old-fashioned is the most commonly chosen incorrect answer, due to confusion with *passé*, which looks and sounds much like BLASÉ.

DEFILE (di-fIl′ or dE-fIl′) v.: to make dirty, corrupt, pollute

To DEFILE something is to make it dirty or impure. DEFILE is a very strong word and suggests doing foul things to something that should be kept pure or sacred.

> "A madman DEFILED the statue by pouring garbage all over it."
>
> "He said his home was being DEFILED by the presence of such a vicious person, and he demanded that the man leave immediately."

BANAL (bA′-nəl or bə-nal′) adj.: commonplace, trite, worn-out

Something that is BANAL lacks all freshness or originality. It is commonplace and uninteresting.

> "The speaker's BANAL remarks put everyone to sleep."
>
> "The plot of the novel was quite BANAL; I've read the same sort of thing a hundred times before."
>
> "All her ideas are BANAL; she hasn't had an original thought in her life."

Many people choose *annoying* as the meaning of BANAL. This may be due to confusion of BANAL with *bane*. A *bane* is something that causes trouble or ruin. It is not related to the word BANAL.

Other forms of the word: BANALITY, n.

EXONERATE (eg-zon′-ə-rAt) v.: to free from blame, clear, relieve

EXONERATE comes from a Latin word meaning "to relieve of a burden." Occasionally EXONERATE is used to mean "to relieve of a task or duty."

> "No one can EXONERATE you from your duty to your parents."

The word is usually used, though, in the sense "to free from the burden of blame."

> "The witness's testimony completely EXONERATED you."
>
> "They admitted the evidence seemed to EXONERATE him from any blame for the fire."

EXONERATE gives the idea not only that the person is not guilty, but that he has been cleared so completely that all the burden of being suspected and accused falls away from him.

Exercise 1

Answer each question with a YES or NO. Put a check in the space for YES or NO next to each question.

		Yes	No
EXAMPLE	Is a speck of dust TINY?	✓	
1.	Do sailors usually have an AFFINITY for the sea?		
2.	Would a VISTA be very close to a person?		
3.	Do some people ASPIRE after fame?		
4.	Can your body ASSIMILATE rocks?		
5.	Could a push give something IMPETUS?		
6.	Would an ARDENT swimmer enjoy going to the beach?		
7.	Do people usually enjoy being CONFOUNDED?		
8.	Would a team REVEL after it had won a championship?		
9.	Are BESTIAL people usually likable?		
10.	Is eating dessert an ORDEAL for most people?		
11.	Would an AFFABLE person frighten most people?		
12.	Would a BLASÉ person get excited very easily?		
13.	Would a person dislike seeing his church DEFILED?		
14.	Would a BANAL play be fascinating to watch?		
15.	If someone was suspected of murder, would he like to be EXONERATED?		

Exercise 2

Each sentence contains a test word in CAPITAL letters. Decide whether the test word is being used correctly or incorrectly in the sentence. Put a check in the space for RIGHT or WRONG next to the sentence

		Right	Wrong
EXAMPLE	After working hard all day Bill felt TINY and wanted to sleep.		✓
1.	The stars seemed to go on and on into AFFINITY.		
2.	These inventions opened up for us wonderful VISTAS of mankind's future.		
3.	He ASPIRED to be a writer, but he ended up working in a factory instead.		
4.	They were able to ASSIMILATE the new students into the class without any problem.		
5.	The project lost all its IMPETUS when Susan quit.		
6.	He shrugged ARDENTLY and said he didn't care much one way or the other.		
7.	The two men CONFOUNDED the business together and have been partners ever since.		

		Right	Wrong
8.	It seemed as if everyone were joining in the noisy REVELS celebrating the end of the war.	______	______
9.	You must all be on your BESTIAL behavior when we meet the principal.	______	______
10.	The man claimed that walking home through the blizzard wasn't an ORDEAL, it was just a minor inconvenience.	______	______
11.	Jim was not very AFFABLE at the party; he sat in a corner and refused to speak to anyone.	______	______
12.	This waltz is so BLASÉ. You should be learning all the modern dances.	______	______
13.	He DEFILED us to come out and fight him.	______	______
14.	The BANAL poison killed them both.	______	______
15.	The judge EXONERATED the man and set him free.	______	______

Exercise 3

Each test word is followed by three other words. Decide which of the three words is LEAST CLOSELY RELATED in its meaning to the meaning of the test word. Put the letter for the word you choose in the space at the end of the line.

EXAMPLE

	TINY:	a) small	b) short	c) angry	C
1.	AFFINITY:	a) liking	b) increase	c) resemblance	______
2.	VISTA:	a) distance	b) smallness	c) view	______
3.	ASPIRE:	a) remember	b) desire	c) hope	______
4.	ASSIMILATE:	a) blend	b) adopt	c) increase	______
5.	IMPETUS:	a) power	b) height	c) force	______
6.	ARDENT:	a) tight	b) fiery	c) strong	______
7.	CONFOUND:	a) excite	b) bewilder	c) puzzle	______
8.	REVEL:	a) delight	b) expect	c) enjoy	______
9.	BESTIAL:	a) crude	b) sad	c) vicious	______
10.	ORDEAL:	a) difficulty	b) pain	c) surprise	______
11.	AFFABLE:	a) friendly	b) beautiful	c) approachable	______
12.	BLASÉ:	a) nonchalant	b) bored	c) ill	______
13.	DEFILE:	a) endanger	b) corrupt	c) dirty	______
14.	BANAL:	a) stale	b) strange	c) dull	______
15.	EXONERATE:	a) free	b) reward	c) relieve	______

Review Test 4—Chapters 10–12

Fill in each blank with the test word (or a form of the test word) which best fits the sentence. Use the words listed below.

AFFABLE	BANAL	EXODUS	ORDEAL	RECAPITULATE
AFFINITY	BESTIAL	IMBIBE	PALPITATE	SORDID
AGGRIEVED	CONFOUND	IMPETUS	PICAYUNE	VISTA
ARDENT	EMPHATIC	MATRON	PLEBEIAN	WILE
ASPIRE				

1. With a(n) ____________ shake of his head he said he would never agree.
2. The three ____________ were dignified ladies who ruled high society for many years.
3. It was a(n) ____________ speech, full of trite phrases and secondhand ideas.
4. Your ____________ behavior will not be tolerated; we don't live in the jungle, you know.
5. Through the long gallery he saw a pleasant ____________ of a garden with a fountain in the middle.
6. His ____________ behavior convinced everyone that he was immoral.
7. She had a couple of ____________ complaints about the meal. She said the onions were cut the wrong way and the napkin was on the wrong side of the plate.
8. He ____________ a great deal of liquor at the party.
9. Whenever he ran too fast his heart would start to ____________.
10. The prisoner used all his ____________ in trying to escape.
11. The nobleman didn't want his son engaging in a(n) ____________ activity like going to the circus. He thought such things were just for common people.
12. His ____________ desire for peace made him work night and day to end the war.
13. There was little ____________ between the two people; they had almost nothing in common.
14. I don't have time to repeat the whole thing so I'll just ____________ the main points.
15. Jim was so shy that it was quite a(n) ____________ for him to ask a girl for a date.
16. Bob felt ____________ when everyone else got to go to the picnic except him.
17. Susan ____________ to be a reporter, so she majored in journalism in college.
18. The governor tried to stop the ____________ of businesses from his state by lowering taxes.
19. All the teachers thought Hal was stupid, but he ____________ everyone by placing first on the exam.
20. Uncle Bill is very ____________; he always has a kind word for you and will listen to all your problems.
21. Our work was starting to slow down, but then it received a new ____________ when several people said they wanted to help.

Fill in each blank with the test word (or a form of the test word) which best fits the sentence. Use the words listed below.

ASSIMILATE	EQUITY	ILLUSTRIOUS	LAUDABLE	SCATHING
BLASÉ	ESPOUSE	IMPART	LEGACY	SUPERFICIAL
CULPABLE	EXONERATE	IMPLEMENT	PALATABLE	WANTON
DEFILE	GINGERLY	INCEPTION	RETICENT	WROUGHT
DISCREET	HEW	INTREPID	REVEL	

22. It is impossible to ____________ all the information contained in this book. There's just too much of it.

23. During the quarrel, she made several ____________ remarks about his driving ability.

24. Rising from humble beginnings be became one of our most ____________ leaders.

25. You must be more ____________; you shouldn't tell everyone all our secrets.

26. He bought us a pair of fine hand-____________ bookends for Christmas.

27. The ____________ soldiers fought their way through enemy territory to rescue the town.

28. Everyone praised the ____________ of his decision, in which each person got what he deserved.

29. When they hear his brilliant speech, I am sure they will ____________ his position on taxes.

30. He ____________ in being the center of attention. Nothing gives him more enjoyment.

31. The wise man ____________ to them the wisdom of the ages.

32. Everyone was shocked by the ____________ destruction of school property; the person who did it obviously wanted to do as much damage as possible.

33. She walked in a(n) ____________ fashion through the room, afraid she would step on one of Billy's toys.

34. They found several stone ____________ which the ancient tribe must have used in farming.

35. He swung his ax and ____________ the large post in two.

36. I am confident this new evidence will completely ____________ the defendant.

37. Her knowledge of the subject was only ____________. She knew a lot of facts, but her understanding of them wasn't very deep.

38. The meat wasn't very good, but at least it was ____________; I couldn't even eat the rest of the meal.

39. His attempts to bring peace to the world are ____________, even if he doesn't succeed.

40. Mary was very ____________ about getting the scholarship. I guess she knew she deserved it.

41. His rich grandfather left him a substantial ____________, so he never has to work again.

42. She ____________ the beautiful church by scrawling filthy words on its wall.

43. Since the ____________ of the new system there have been far fewer problems.

44. The landlord was ____________ in this accident, because he hadn't fixed the stairway after he had been ordered to.

45. The ____________ girl couldn't bring herself to tell the boy how much she liked him.

Common Prefixes

A *prefix* is one or more syllables placed at the beginning of a word that change or add to its meaning. Only some of the more common prefixes have been listed here. Note that many prefixes have more than one spelling. Also note that prefixes may have more than one meaning. Only the most important ones are given here; check your dictionary for other meanings.

Prefix	Meaning	Examples
A-, also AN-	not; without	ANonymous: without a name
AB-, also ABS-	away from	ABsent: away, not present
AD-, also A followed by two consonants	to; toward	ADhere: to stick to ATTract: to pull toward
ANTI-	against	ANTIslavery: against slavery
CON-, also COM-, COL-, CO-, COR-	with; together	CONnect: to join together COMbine: to mix together
DE-	down from; away from; not	DEpart: to go away DEpress: to press down on, make sad
DIS-, also DI-	apart; away; not	DISmiss: to send away DIShonest: not honest
EX-, also E-	out of; from	EXclaim: to shout out Emerge: to come out
1. IN-, also IL-, IM-, IR-	in; into	INsert: to put in IMport: to bring into (a country)
2. IN-, also IL-, IM-, IR-	not	INformal: not formal ILlegal: not legal
INTER-	between; among	INTERrupt: to break into the middle of INTERnational: among nations
MIS-	badly; wrong; not	MIStreat: to treat badly MIStake: a wrong answer
NON-	not	NONbeliever: not a believer NONstop: not stopping

Prefix	Meaning	Examples
PRE-	before; early; in advance	PREpare: to get ready beforehand PREhistoric: before history
PRO-	in front of; forward; in favor of	PROceed: to go forward PROminent: standing out; easily seen
RE-	back; again	REfund: to pay back REsume: to begin again
SUB-	under; below	SUBmarine: a ship that can travel under water
SUPER-	over; above; beyond	SUPERvise: to watch over SUPERhuman: beyond human strength or ability
TRANS-, also TRA-	across; beyond; through	TRANSparent: able to be seen through TRANSoceanic: crossing the ocean; beyond the ocean
UN-	not; opposite of	UNhappy: not happy UNlock: to do the opposite of locking

Common Suffixes

A *suffix* is one or more syllables added to the end of a word to change or add to its meaning. As with the prefix list, only the more common ones have been listed here. Note that an important job of a suffix—and sometimes its only job—is to show the part of speech of the word to which it is attached.

Suffix	Meaning	Examples	Part of Speech
-ABLE, also -IBLE	able to; tending to; having	breakABLE: able to be broken valuABLE: having value	adjective
-AL	connected with; like	originAL: connected with the beginning monumentAL: like a monument	adjective
-ANT, also -ENT	doing; being	pleasANT: being pleasing differENT: not being the same	adjective
1. -ATE	to make; to act; to cause	abbreviATE: to make shorter activATE: to cause to become active	verb
2. -ATE	being	adequATE: being enough	adjective
-ER, also -OR	one that is; one that does	foreignER: one who is foreign actOR: one who acts	noun
-FUL	full of; able to	beautiFUL: full of beauty harmFUL: able to harm	adjective
-FY, also -IFY	to make; to cause; to be	simplIFY: to make simple liqueFY: to make liquid	verb
-IC, also -ICAL	like; being	metallIC: being metal fanatICAL: like a fanatic	adjective
-ISH	like; somewhat	childISH: like a child reddISH: somewhat red	adjective
-ITY	a state; condition	insanITY: the state of being insane	noun
-IVE	connected with; having a tendency toward	actIVE: tending to be full of action festIVE: like a festival	adjective

Suffix	Meaning	Examples	Part of Speech
-LESS	without; unable to be done	fatherLESS: without a father countLESS: unable to be counted	adjective
-MENT	a state; condition; result	amazeMENT: the state of being amazed attachMENT: the result of attaching	noun
-NESS	a quality; state	darkNESS: the state of being dark goodNESS: the quality of being good	noun
-OUS	full of; having; like	courageOUS: having courage joyOUS: full of joy	adjective
-TUDE	a state; condition	gratiTUDE: the state of being thankful	noun
-Y	full of; having; inclined to	greedY: full of greed dreamY: inclined to dream	adjective

Answers—WORDBOOK 6

Chapter 1

		Pretest	Exercise 1	Exercise 2	Exercise 3
1.	LEVY:	impose	N	R	a
2.	ONSLAUGHT:	attack	Y	R	b
3.	THWART:	block	N	R	c
4.	DEGENERATE:	worsen	N	W	b
5.	ELITE:	chosen	N	R	a
6.	INDIFFERENT:	uninterested	N	R	a
7.	KALEIDOSCOPIC:	continually changing	Y	W	b
8.	PATERNAL:	fatherly	Y	W	a
9.	RETROSPECT:	review	N	R	b
10.	TORRENT:	flood	Y	W	c
11.	ZENITH:	peak	Y	R	c
12.	BIGOTED:	intolerant	N	R	c
13.	EXCEPTIONAL:	unusual	Y	W	a
14.	IMPERATIVE:	urgent	N	R	c
15.	PERCEIVE:	notice	Y	R	c

Chapter 2

1.	IMPAIR:	weakened	Y	W	b
2.	SYNOPSIS:	summary	N	R	a
3.	BLISS:	joy	Y	R	a
4.	INFRINGE:	broke	N	R	b
5.	MICROBE:	germ	Y	R	c
6.	NONENTITY:	unimportant person	N	R	b
7.	TREMULOUS:	quivering	Y	R	c
8.	VOID:	emptiness	Y	W	a
9.	ASSAIL:	attacked	N	R	c
10.	HYPOCRISY:	insincerity	N	R	c
11.	DESTITUTE:	poor	N	R	c
12.	ENDOW:	provided	N	R	c
13.	IMBECILIC:	idiotic	N	W	c
14.	LOATH:	unwilling	N	R	a
15.	THRONG:	crowd	N	R	a

Chapter 3

1.	CAVORT:	make merry	N	R	b
2.	CONCEDE:	admit	N	R	c
3.	INTEGRAL:	essential	Y	R	b
4.	DOTING:	overly fond	Y	W	a
5.	INTERIM:	temporary	N	R	a
6.	LACKLUSTER:	dull	N	R	c
7.	CONVULSION:	fit	N	R	b
8.	PLAUSIBLE:	likely	Y	R	c
9.	WHIMSICAL:	playful	Y	W	a
10.	ABORIGINE:	natives	N	R	c
11.	CEREBRAL:	mental	N	W	a
12.	INCITE:	stir up	Y	W	b
13.	COSMOPOLITAN:	worldwide	N	R	c
14.	DERIVATION:	source	Y	R	a
15.	FRACAS:	fight	Y	R	c

Chapter 4

		Pretest	Exercise 1	Exercise 2	Exercise 3
1.	MANIFOLD:	numerous	N	R	b
2.	QUIRK:	peculiarity	N	R	c
3.	NONPAREIL:	unequaled	Y	R	a
4.	PANG:	pains	N	R	b
5.	SWOON:	faint	N	R	c
6.	HALLOWED:	holy	Y	W	b
7.	IMPLORE:	begged	Y	R	c
8.	PROCURE:	obtain	N	R	b
9.	ALLOT:	assigned	Y	R	c
10.	BLASPHEME:	curse	N	R	b
11.	MELEE:	free-for-all	N	R	a
12.	PLACATE:	soothe	N	R	a
13.	VEHEMENT:	intense	Y	W	c
14.	STEADFAST:	loyal	N	W	a
15.	ALOOF:	distant	N	R	a

Chapter 5

		Pretest	Exercise 1	Exercise 2	Exercise 3
1.	BENEVOLENT:	kindly	N	W	a
2.	GUISE:	appearance	Y	R	b
3.	CONTRIVE:	invent	Y	R	b
4.	DEPICT:	describe	Y	R	b
5.	JAUNDICED:	yellowish	N	R	c
6.	PENSIVE:	thoughtful	N	R	a
7.	SQUANDER:	wastes	N	R	b
8.	ULTERIOR:	hidden	Y	W	c
9.	AMASS:	gather	Y	R	a
10.	KINDRED:	related	Y	W	c
11.	ORDINANCE:	orders	Y	W	b
12.	KNOLL:	small hill	N	R	b
13.	ORIFICE:	opening	Y	W	b
14.	QUASH:	crush	N	W	b
15.	SLOVENLY:	untidy	N	R	a

Chapter 6

		Pretest	Exercise 1	Exercise 2	Exercise 3
1.	FACADE:	front	Y	R	c
2.	ADULTERATE:	made impure	N	R	c
3.	CLEAVE:	split	Y	W	c
4.	ENUMERATE:	listed	N	R	c
5.	AFFIX:	fastened	Y	W	a
6.	PRECIPICE:	cliff	Y	W	a
7.	AGAPE:	wide-open	Y	R	c
8.	SUBMISSIVE:	tame	Y	W	c
9.	ANTAGONISM:	hostility	N	W	a
10.	APPENDAGE:	attachment	N	R	a
11.	DOMICILE:	home	N	R	b
12.	GUFFAW:	noisy laugh	N	R	a
13.	STRATA:	layers	N	R	a
14.	BUFFOON:	clown	Y	R	b
15.	ADVOCATE:	recommend	Y	R	a

Chapter 7

		Pretest	Exercise 1	Exercise 2	Exercise 3
1.	DESPOT:	tyrant	N	R	a
2.	GENTEEL:	polite	N	R	a
3.	INSUBORDINATE:	disobedient	N	R	b
4.	GIRTH:	size	Y	R	c
5.	INTERJECTION:	exclamation	Y	W	b
6.	REBUKE:	scold	N	R	b
7.	LISTLESS:	spiritless	N	W	c
8.	PARAPHERNALIA:	equipment	Y	R	b
9.	REPERCUSSION:	effects	Y	W	b
10.	VIABLE:	workable	N	R	b
11.	BAUBLE:	trinkets	N	R	a
12.	ATTAIN:	reach	Y	W	c
13.	BERATE:	scolded	N	R	c
14.	CONSENSUS:	agreement	Y	W	a
15.	IMPASSIVE:	unmoved	N	R	c

Chapter 8

		Pretest	Exercise 1	Exercise 2	Exercise 3
1.	SAGE:	wise	N	R	a
2.	INDULGE:	pamper	N	R	b
3.	RECTIFY:	correct	Y	W	c
4.	INSURRECTION:	uprising	Y	W	c
5.	REPREHENSIBLE:	blameworthy	N	W	b
6.	SOLACE:	comfort	Y	W	c
7.	MEMOIRS	life story	Y	R	a
8.	RECOMPENSE:	reward	N	W	a
9.	TINGE:	trace	Y	R	b
10.	VANQUISH:	defeat	N	R	b
11.	BREVITY:	shortness	N	R	b
12.	VENDETTA:	blood feud	N	R	a
13.	DELETE:	erase	Y	R	a
14.	MIRTH:	merriment	N	R	b
15.	RABBLE:	mob	Y	R	b

Chapter 9

		Pretest	Exercise 1	Exercise 2	Exercise 3
1.	SMUG:	self-satisfied	N	R	c
2.	VINDICTIVE:	vengeful	Y	R	a
3.	BEDEVIL:	torment	N	R	c
4.	NEGLIGIBLE:	unimportant	N	R	a
5.	EDIFYING:	uplifting	N	W	b
6.	MALEFACTOR:	criminal	Y	W	a
7.	MUSE:	meditate	Y	W	c
8.	REPROACH:	blame	Y	W	c
9.	ENVOY:	messenger	Y	R	a
10.	FISSURE:	narrow crack	N	R	c
11.	COALESCE:	unite	Y	R	b
12.	DELUGE:	flood	N	R	c
13.	FARCICAL:	absurd	N	R	b
14.	SURMISE:	guess	Y	R	c
15.	ASSENT:	agreed	Y	W	b

Chapter 10

		Pretest	Exercise 1	Exercise 2	Exercise 3
1.	EMPHATIC:	forceful	Y	R	a
2.	INCEPTION:	beginning	N	W	b
3.	GINGERLY:	careful	Y	R	c
4.	IMPLEMENT:	tool	Y	W	a
5.	PALPITATE:	throb	N	W	c
6.	INTREPID:	fearless	Y	W	b
7.	MATRON:	married woman	N	R	b
8.	PALATABLE:	tasty	N	R	a
9.	RETICENT:	quiet	N	R	c
10.	SORDID:	filthy	Y	W	a
11.	DISCREET:	tactful	Y	R	a
12.	AGGRIEVED:	wronged	Y	R	c
13.	EQUITY:	fairness	N	W	c
14.	LEGACY:	inheritance	Y	R	a
15.	PLEBEIAN:	commonplace	N	R	a

Chapter 11

		Pretest	Exercise 1	Exercise 2	Exercise 3
1.	RECAPITULATE:	sum up	Y	R	a
2.	EXODUS:	mass departure	N	R	c
3.	IMBIBE:	drank	Y	W	c
4.	HEW:	cut	Y	R	a
5.	ILLUSTRIOUS:	famous	N	R	a
6.	WANTON:	immoral	N	R	b
7.	IMPART:	make known	Y	R	a
8.	WILE:	tricks	N	R	b
9.	ESPOUSE:	supports	N	R	c
10.	WROUGHT:	shaped	N	W	a
11.	LAUDABLE:	praiseworthy	Y	W	b
12.	CULPABLE:	blameworthy	Y	W	b
13.	PICAYUNE:	trivial	N	W	b
14.	SCATHING:	damaging	N	R	b
15.	SUPERFICIAL:	shallow	N	W	c

Chapter 12

		Pretest	Exercise 1	Exercise 2	Exercise 3
1.	AFFINITY:	attraction	Y	W	b
2.	VISTA:	view	N	R	b
3.	ASPIRE:	long	Y	R	a
4.	ASSIMILATE:	absorbed	N	R	c
5.	IMPETUS:	moving force	Y	R	b
6.	ARDENT:	burning	Y	W	a
7.	CONFOUND:	confuse	N	W	a
8.	REVEL:	make merry	Y	R	b
9.	BESTIAL:	animal-like	N	W	b
10.	ORDEAL:	severe trial	N	R	c
11.	AFFABLE:	pleasant	N	R	b
12.	BLASÉ:	indifferent	N	W	c
13.	DEFILE:	dirty	Y	W	a
14.	BANAL:	commonplace	N	W	b
15.	EXONERATED:	cleared	Y	R	b

Review Test 1

1. hypocrisy
2. elite
3. degenerated
4. imbecilic
5. bigoted
6. convulsions
7. infringes
8. doting
9. loath
10. torrent
11. assailed
12. indifferent
13. conceded
14. nonentity
15. fracas
16. cerebral
17. throng
18. aborigines
19. destitute
20. integral
21. plausible
22. perceive
23. endow
24. interim
25. incited
26. zenith
27. synopsis
28. derivation
29. impaired
30. exceptional
31. onslaught
32. cavorted
33. bliss
34. retrospect
35. paternal
36. levied
37. whimsical
38. lackluster
39. tremulous
40. kaleidoscopic
41. void
42. cosmopolitan
43. thwart
44. microbe
45. imperative

Review Test 2

1. kindred
2. strata
3. steadfast
4. squandered
5. swooned
6. vehement
7. submissive
8. contrived
9. placate
10. blasphemed
11. guffaws
12. pang
13. quirk
14. agape
15. domicile
16. pensive
17. aloof
18. orifice
19. melee
20. benevolent
21. manifold
22. hallowed
23. procure
24. cleave
25. advocated
26. buffoons
27. adulterated
28. jaundiced
29. facade
30. enumerate
31. slovenly
32. quash
33. allotted
34. precipice
35. depicted
36. appendage
37. antagonism
38. amassed
39. affixed
40. implored
41. nonpareil
42. guise
43. ulterior
44. knoll
45. ordinance

Review Test 3

1. impassive
2. reproached
3. vanquish
4. malefactor
5. muse
6. insubordinate
7. rectify
8. memoirs
9. mirth
10. girth
11. brevity
12. viable
13. vendetta
14. berated
15. insurrections
16. deleted
17. paraphernalia
18. deluge
19. bauble
20. sage
21. tinge
22. bedeviled
23. recompense
24. attain
25. reprehensible
26. edifying
27. rabble
28. rebuked
29. listless
30. surmise
31. consensus
32. negligible
33. envoy
34. farcical
35. assented
36. repercussions
37. fissure
38. vindictive
39. indulged
40. genteel
41. smug
42. coalesced
43. despot
44. solace
45. interjections

Review Test 4

1. emphatic
2. matrons
3. banal
4. bestial
5. vista
6. sordid
7. picayune
8. imbibed
9. palpitate
10. wiles
11. plebeian
12. ardent
13. affinity
14. recapitulate
15. ordeal
16. aggrieved
17. aspired
18. exodus
19. confounded
20. affable
21. impetus
22. assimilate
23. scathing
24. illustrious
25. discreet
26. wrought
27. intrepid
28. equity
29. espouse
30. revels
31. imparted
32. wanton
33. gingerly
34. implements
35. hewed
36. exonerate
37. superficial
38. palatable
39. laudable
40. blasé
41. legacy
42. defiled
43. inception
44. culpable
45. reticent

Index—WORDBOOK 6

The number after each word indicates the chapter in which the word is treated.

Vocabulary Review List

On this page you can list words from the *Wordbook* that gave you particular difficulty, so that you can continue to review them. You might also wish to include in the list difficult words that you come across in your reading. The sample sentence may be one you make up yourself, a sentence from the *Wordbook* discussion, or a sentence from your reading. It should clearly illustrate how the word is used. This page can be removed from the *Wordbook* and placed in a notebook or three-ring binder for easy reference.

Word	**Definition**	**Sample Sentence**
FUTILE	useless, ineffective	He made a FUTILE attempt to push the car by himself, then gave up.

Word	Definition	Sample Sentence